SOCIAL STORIES FOR KIDS IN CONFLICT

SECOND EDITION

JOHN LING

Routledge
Taylor & Francis Group

LONDON AND NEW YORK

Second edition published 2017
by Routledge
2 Park Square, Milton Park, Abingdon, Oxon OX14 4RN

and by Routledge
711 Third Avenue, New York, NY 10017

Routledge is an imprint of the Taylor & Francis Group, an informa business

First edition published by Speechmark Publishing 2010

British Library Cataloguing-in-Publication Data
A catalogue record for this book is available from the British Library

Library of Congress Cataloging-in-Publication Data
A catalog record for this book has been requested.

ISBN: 978-1-91118-602-1 (pbk)
ISBN: 978-1-31517-499-0 (ebk)

Typeset in Signa Condensed
by MooCreative (Luton)

Activate your accompanying online resources
- Go to www.routledge.com/cw/speechmark then click on the cover of this book
- Click the 'Sign in or Request Access' button and follow the instructions, in order to access your accompanying online resources

Printed in the United Kingdom by CMP (uk) Limited

CONTENTS

AUTHOR'S ACKNOWLEDGEMENTS

My thanks to all the young people I have worked with over the years who have helped me to create and develop the ideas in this book. I hope they are pleased with the results and feel proud that our discussions will help many young people in the future.

Thanks also to Pete Forde, Educational Psychologist, who has made many helpful suggestions for this revised second edition.

John Ling
July 2016

INTRODUCTION

This book will help people who work and/or live with young people who have difficulties with their behaviour and relationships with others. It has developed from work with young people who have autism, Asperger syndrome and related conditions such as Tourette syndrome and ADHD (attention deficit hyperactivity disorder). However, the ideas and techniques described here can be used to help all young people to become more aware of their behaviour and its effect on other people.

The book is divided into three parts, the first two being techniques to use with young people.

- Part 1 Social stories

- Part 2 Cartoons and other visual techniques which can be used to present alternative ways to discuss problems.

- Part 3 Context

There is also a PowerPoint presentation in the accompanying online resources. This can be used with staff members, parents and carers to introduce the ideas presented in this book.

First, start by reading the first section of Part 3, 'Setting the contents in a real context', to see how the ideas have developed and then dip into the relevant sections. The subject index (page 13) will help you to find cartoons or social stories that might be useful when you are in a situation with a young person, at home or at school, and you don't know what to do.

In this new edition of the book, the social stories have been extended, using material from the 'dialogues' in the first edition. Please note that 'he' and 'him' are used when referring to the child to keep the language simple.

STRUCTURE OF THE BOOK

The book has two main sections devoted to working with young people:

- Social stories

- Cartoons and other visual techniques.

These require a meaningful discussion with either the child or their peers and/or their families. My work with these groups has been greatly influenced by my work as a mediator.

The online resources, which can be downloaded, printed and copied, are described at the end of this introduction, along with details of where to find them.

Social stories

These stories were written for the benefit of individual children with autism in schools in Kirklees, UK. Many of them were written either with or by the child or by their teacher or helper. They should also prove helpful for many other children with or without autism. I hope they will be of great practical use to both school staff and parents. You may copy individual stories, but I hope you will use them as a model or starting point for your own because each one has to be tailored to your individual child.

Social stories work best if they are 'owned' by the child. You may use a model from the book, but it is best if you and the child agree on what it should contain, and even better if you write it together. Use pictures if you can draw, or get them from Clip Art, from the internet (for example, Google images), or photographs.If parents or carers know what you are aiming to do, they can help by doing the same at home. So make sure that they have a copy of the social stories. It also helps if the child understands that both school and parents are working together.

The other children in the class or family also need to know what the child is trying to achieve. They can be helpful in reminding the child and reinforcing the desired behaviour.

The social stories need to be practical and achievable. Stick to down-to-earth language such as the child might use. It is not a teacher telling the child what to do, but the child telling himself.

The social stories don't always have to be about bad things that you want to change. You can also write them to celebrate good things.

Note that there are almost no negative statements. Try to say what you want to achieve using only positives. By working on the positive outcome, it is sometimes possible to ignore or diminish the negative behaviour.

Make the story part of a daily routine or even more frequent. Read it with the child just before starting the activity. For example, if it is about putting your hand up and not calling out the answers, read it just before that activity is to begin. If it is about making a fuss in the supermarket, read it just before setting off. If the behaviour has already occurred, take the child aside and read the social story again, then return to the activity.

When the child has achieved the desired behaviour, celebrate it with a small reward or praise from you and the other children. Alternatively, set up the reward just before the activity begins so that he knows what he is aiming for.

Keep the social stories in a folder along with other key items such as photographs, rewards, and so on. Then the child can look at it often and reinforce his behaviour.

When the behaviour has been achieved, stop using the social stories, but keep them in the folder, so that you can just point to them occasionally as a reminder.

Social story scenarios

Below are some examples of typical situations that might be suitable for a social story intervention.

- Elizabeth is 12. She is very anxious to please and deeply worried all day long that she might not keep up with other students in her work. When the teacher says 'Five minutes left', she panics and can't make herself finish because she thinks she has not done enough.

- Abdul is five and in Year 1. He loves playing on the bikes in the playground and, at playtime, he rushes out to get one before anyone else. There are only six bikes and 25 children. He plays all the time on one bike and gets mad if another child or a teacher tries to prise him off it.

- Suzie is 14 and loves books. She has been made a library monitor in her school, partly because of this and partly to avoid being bullied in the playground. She likes to have rules for everything and gets upset if other children don't stick to them. Once, she was so keen to keep some students out of the library when it was time to close, she squashed a girl's head in the door.

- Joe is six and loves being at school so much that he can't bear it to end. At the end of the day, when it is time to go home and the children are let out of class, he runs across the playground to his mother and hits her repeatedly.

- Daniel is eight and loves to play football. At break time, he rushes out to get one of the school balls. When he is joined by some other boys, he likes to kick penalties all the time. If he does not get a ball, he tries to butt into other boys' games and take the ball off to kick a penalty. If he is in the middle of a game and someone tackles him successfully, he flies into a rage and runs away.

- Joe is 13 and a computer wizard. During IT lessons, he looks at other students' work on the screen and, if they are having difficulty, he tells them how to do it right. Some of them resent this.

Writing a social story

The planning sheet on page 12 provides a framework to help you plan a social story.

The social stories in Part 1 are grouped under the following headings:

- Personal stuff
- Daily routines
- Home life
- Social skills
- Homework
- School work
- Playtime, PE (physical education) and games

The subject index on page 13 will guide you to the following specific topics in the social stories (SS).

Personal stuff (SS1–18)

This is where school and domestic issues overlap. For example, toileting is a perennial issue and some children carry problems from infancy well into the junior years, and even into senior school. Unfortunately, in the UK, the toilets in secondary schools have had a bad reputation for many years and some schools now recognise the need for privacy and safety. Children can see school toilets as threatening because the locks do not work or because they are not supervised (SS16 and 24).

A few children continue to explore their bodily functions in public without realising how embarrassing this can be to others. Some forget that nudity is OK for little children but not in front of adolescent peers. Some parents are too embarrassed to deal with certain issues and some of the other children are embarrassed but don't know how to deal with their friend who picks his nose or strokes his penis.

If a child is insensitive to other people's feelings, it is often possible to speak very bluntly to them about a problem because they are less likely to be upset than children who are more sensitive. Failing that, a social story might be just the thing.

Daily routines (SS19–26)

Many of these routines are covered in my first book (Ling, 2010), including toilet routines, washing, queuing, sitting and standing, playtime, mealtime, going home, school work and PE. This section contains a few more ideas.

It is a cliché that all children like to stay within well-known routines. Children with autism, Asperger's, ADHD and some other conditions only feel secure within a known routine. Life in school is subject to many sudden changes – absent teachers, absent friends, unexpected visitors, trips out, fire alarms, and so on – so life for some children is one long round of anxiety.

One of the best ways to help these children, and many others, is to use a visual timetable, either individually or for the whole class. This consists of several card symbols, one for each regular activity, for example, assembly, reading time, break time, plus a few made up on the day. These are stuck on a card strip with Velcro® in the order they occur. The used and unused ones are kept in a wallet nearby.

For infants, another copy of the symbol cards is attached to the place or object to which it refers, for example, the sandpit and the toilet. As the routine changes from one activity to the next, the child takes the next card from the strip and takes it to the place where the matching card is. The previous card is put into the wallet.

For older children, the routine can be displayed either on the board or on the child's desk. Even older children appreciate a written list of activities taking place during the day or during an individual lesson. This helps them to do things in the right order and avoid getting confused about what happens next. Give the child responsibility by asking the very useful question, 'What do you have to do next?'

Home life (SS27–31)

Sometimes there is a whole other set of problems at home and elsewhere because some children like to keep home and school in separate boxes. Parents often tell me about a list of problems that teachers don't encounter in school. It helps to know what goes on at home, for three reasons.

1 The child does not realise that adults talk to each other about them.

2 One often throws light on the other.

3 It helps for everyone involved with the child to use the same strategies.

Social skills (SS32–70)

Social skills is the area of life that most children are never taught as such. They pick it up by learning from others around them and as part of an ongoing daily agenda in the classroom. For example, we don't think we have to teach a person to look at us when we talk to them because most people do it from being a baby.

Smiling when we are praised should come naturally. Attention-seeking behaviour is encouraged in babies but, as we get older, we learn it is not so welcome. However, some children don't have these built-in instincts. For them, the daily social round is confusing, annoying, frightening even. Knowing when to laugh and when not to, when to touch and when not to, how much is too far when you are hurting or embarrassing someone, and many more social skills, constitute a whole language in itself, which some children find almost impossible to learn.

Homework (SS71–75)

This is a perennial problem for all parents but, for some children, it is one burden too many. Some simply don't understand *why* they have to do school work at home. They will resist, either passively or actively, to the immense frustration of both parents and teachers. And, in the final two years of secondary school, when course work becomes an essential part of the routine, they require a huge amount of help just to get organised from day to day. Let's face it: some people will *never* be organised!

Many senior schools (11–16 year olds in the UK) now provide homework clubs by one name or another, but not many primary schools (5–11 year olds in the UK). Some schools also recognise that the full curriculum is just too much for some children to handle. Instead, they are allowed to work to a reduced curriculum, so that the course work and homework can be fitted in without too much stress.

Some children cannot explain to their parents what they have to do for homework. Others will stop at the first problem. Some will work for hours on a piece of work that is meant to last 20 minutes. Others will be unable to ask for help from a friend or a member of staff because sometimes they don't realise that another person may be a part of the solution.

I always say to parents, if he can't do it and you can't understand it, don't fret – just write a note to the teacher. It is the teacher's responsibility to make things clear to the child. And to teachers I say, if you leave it until the last minute to set homework, and don't write it down clearly, this child will probably forget what to do. Make it explicit and, if possible, visual.

School work (SS76–100)

Most schools, especially junior and infant schools, make work seem like a pleasant way to pass the time, and most children are happy to do it. However, some just cannot understand *why* they have to do it, or the act of doing it brings up a host of problems. For example:

- Why do I have to do this?

- Why do I have to do it again?

- I can do it in my head, so why bother writing it down?

- Practise? What for?

- I'm a perfectionist!

- I'm not working for *her*!

- I can't get started!

- I like doodling.

- I'm a daydreamer.

- Why is my work different to everyone else's?

- What do I do when I've finished?

- Help, I haven't finished!

- Why has he got a reward but not me?

- What happens if I don't do it?

You might need to remember that school is an artificial construction for keeping children occupied and bears only a faint resemblance to real life. We think we all understand and agree with what goes on in there. But, thank goodness, this is not obvious to every child. Bring on the dissenters!

Playtime, PE and games (SS101–106)

For some children, playtime, PE or games can be the most stressful time of the week, especially in senior school. It is good to see that many PE teachers are now more sensitive to the fears and difficulties created by this part of the school routine. Problems include:

- noise in the changing rooms

- teasing and bullying in the changing rooms

- taking your clothes off

- getting in a muddle with your clothes

- teachers shouting

- being cold

- not understanding the rules of games
- being unable to work in a team
- not understanding why we do sports at all
- not being picked for a team
- being clumsy and slow
- being left out of games
- spoiling other children's games.

Some schools can provide small-scale activities for children who don't like being in 'big' games such as football. Some schools are prepared to allow the child to watch or keep score, or to do other jobs until they feel ready to join in. And some children are prepared to watch out for the awkward child and help them along without getting cross.

Cartoons and other visual techniques

Sometimes people say to me, 'I keep on telling him, but he keeps on doing it.' And I say, 'You told him, but did you show him?'

One time I was observing a boy from outside his classroom. He was a very angry boy. After 10 minutes in the class, he had said something that upset the teacher and was sent out to sit in the shared area near me to calm down. After five minutes, he was calm and went back in.

After another 10 minutes, he was sent out again. The same sequence of events happened three times. After this, the class went into the hall for PE. The boy went to join them, did something unacceptable and was sent out yet again.

This time I decided to intervene. When he was calm, I took out a notepad and together we drew what had been happening using little stickmen pictures with speech bubbles. This in itself is a calming and absorbing exercise. I made no comment on what he had been doing.

At the end of this he said, 'That's bloody stupid, isn't it?' And I said, 'What will we have to draw to make it all right again?' We drew a picture of him going into the hall, saying sorry to the teacher and sitting down quietly. After this, he went into the hall, said sorry to the teacher and sat down quietly. There were no more incidents that afternoon.

I know there isn't always time to do this but, maybe after the incident, you could give it a try. The same idea also applies to harassed parents whose child can't seem to get dressed or washed on time and in the right order. Make lists, draw little picture symbols, stick them on the wall in the bathroom or bedroom, and ask, 'What do you have to do next?'

Sometimes simple visuals present a clearer way for the child to think about problems and how they could be solved. For many children, these are more powerful than lots of words.

Online resources

All of the material in the online resources can be downloaded and printed from the Routledge website at www.routledge.com/cw/speechmark. The pages in this book with the symbol can also be photocopied.

The online resources include:

• the planning sheet
• the PowerPoint presentation.

Choose a situation.

What is the goal?

Gather information. What normally happens?

Give reasons. What happens next?

How does the child usually behave, what effect does this have?

What is the child's goal? Think of a reinforcer.

Think of a title. What kind of picture?

Now try to write your story, tailoring the text to suit the child.

Always end it with a positive statement, such as (I will try ...)

SUBJECT INDEX

This is an index to the cartoons (C) and social stories (SS).

PART 1
SOCIAL STORIES

CONTENTS

School work

Playtime, PE and games

PERSONAL STUFF

1 HOW FRESH IS FRESH?

I like to eat fresh food.

This means to me, just a few minutes after cooking.

If I have to wait too long then I think it isn't fresh any more.

But just how fresh is the food I eat?

Fish and chips. The fish was caught many weeks before it got to the shop and then kept in a freezer. Then it takes … minutes to get from the shop to my house.

Bananas are picked weeks or months before they get to the shop and then kept in cold storage. So when I peel one and eat it straight away, is it fresh?

Eggs can be weeks old when we buy them.

Milk may be up to a week old when we buy it.

When we cook something, the heat kills all the germs.

As long as it stays hot, there will be no germs on it.

Even if it takes fifteen minutes to eat it after cooking, it will still be OK.

Some people might think it is bad manners to eat so quickly after cooking.

If I leave food because I don't think it is fresh, that may also be bad manners.

Do I want to offend the person who cooks the food?

Am I being too picky?

12 NITS

Sometimes I get nits in my hair.

Everyone gets them from time to time.

When they come, I have to wash my hair with some special stuff.

Then my mum has to spend a long time combing my hair.

Then all the little eggs come out.

If we get nits in school, they spread from one child to another.

Nobody likes having nits.

Nobody likes to get close to someone who has nits.

My friends won't like to be too near me if I have nits.

I will make sure my mum helps me to get rid of them.

Then we will all be good friends at school.

13 SOMETIMES I GET TOO CLOSE

Everyone has their own body space.

This is like an invisible balloon around each person. Inside this space, we each feel comfortable.

Some people like a bigger space than others.

But nobody likes anyone else coming inside their body space.

It makes them feel uncomfortable or threatened.

If I sit too close to a friend or a member of school staff, they may feel uncomfortable, especially if my body touches theirs.

Sometimes I don't like it if someone comes inside my body space.

When we love someone, such as our mum or dad, we can have a hug. That is OK because we love each other.

It is OK between special friends.

But it is not OK if the person is not a special friend.

I will try not to sit too close to or touch other people.

Then we will all feel comfortable around each other.

Nobody will be embarrassed.

14 WHAT TO DO WHEN I CAN'T SLEEP

Sometimes I wake up very early.

Things go through my head that frighten me.

Some things go round and round in my head and won't go away.

I don't know what to do about it.

I like to go into my mum's bedroom.

But if she is asleep, she doesn't like to be woken up.

This is not fair on her.

It makes her more tired in the morning.

If I put the TV on, this might wake other people up.

The programmes in the middle of the night are not for young people. Sometimes they can be frightening too.

This is not fair on other people.

Here are some things I can try to do:

- I will not have too much to eat or drink at bedtime.

- I will get myself organised for school early in the evening.

- I will do something nice with Mum or Dad or my brother before we go to bed, like read a story or play a game, or watch a programme together.

- I will read a book in bed if I am awake.

- I will listen to my MP3 player.

- I will cover my head with the quilt.

- I will ask Mum if she will take me to the doctor for some medicine to help me sleep.

- I will try not to go in her room or wake people up.

15 WHEN I WASH MY HAIR

This is what I will do.

1 Stand in the shower and put my head under the water.

2 Rub all of my fingers in my hair to make it wet.

3 Move my head out of the shower.

4 Put a blob of shampoo in one hand.

5 Close my eyes and rub the shampoo into my hair with all of my fingers to make it nice and soapy.

6 Put my head in the shower again.

7 Rub my hair to get rid of all the soap.

Now all of the grease and dirt is washed out of my hair.

8 Start again. Do steps 1 to 7 again.

This makes my hair nice and soft.

9   Wash the rest of my body with soap.

10 Wash the soap off under the shower.

11 Turn off the shower.

12 Get out of the shower.

13 Dry my body with a towel.

14 Rub my hair with the towel a bit longer.

15 Comb my hair.

16 Get dressed.

16 WHEN SHOULD I GO TO THE TOILET?

Everyone goes to the toilet at least once every day.

If we did not, our bowels and bladder would fill up with waste matter and we would be ill.

When I am at school, I forget sometimes about going to the toilet.

I don't like asking to go in front of my fellow students.

This makes me feel uncomfortable.

Sometimes I make a smell, which makes other people feel uncomfortable.

It is OK to go to the toilet in school.

My teachers don't like me to be out of lessons for a long time.

The best time to go is in between lessons.

I will remember to go to the toilet in between lessons.

Then the teachers will be pleased and nobody will feel uncomfortable.

These are the times when it is OK to go to the toilet.

· At home (any time)

· At break time

· At lunchtime

· If I am desperate during lesson time, I can tell the teacher quietly and politely.

17 WHICH BITS OF ME ARE PRIVATE? (BOY)

When I was a little boy, I could take my clothes off and nobody minded.

Now I am a big boy, I have to keep most of my body covered up.

I can show my head and arms and the bottom half of my legs.

But all the rest is private. Only Mum can see those bits.

If I show off my private bits, people will be embarrassed.

It makes them feel uncomfortable.

Colour the private bits red.

Colour the public bits green.

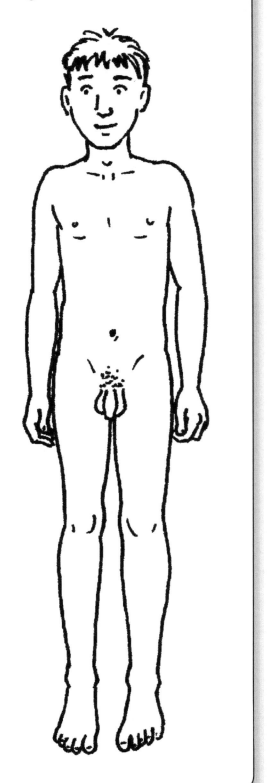

18 WHICH BITS OF ME ARE PRIVATE? (GIRL)

When I was a little girl, I could take my clothes off and nobody minded.

Now I am a big girl, I have to keep most of my body covered up.

I can show my head and arms and the bottom half of my legs.

But all the rest is private. Only Mum can see those bits.

If I show off my private bits, people will be embarrassed.

It makes them feel uncomfortable.

Colour the private bits red.

Colour the public bits green.

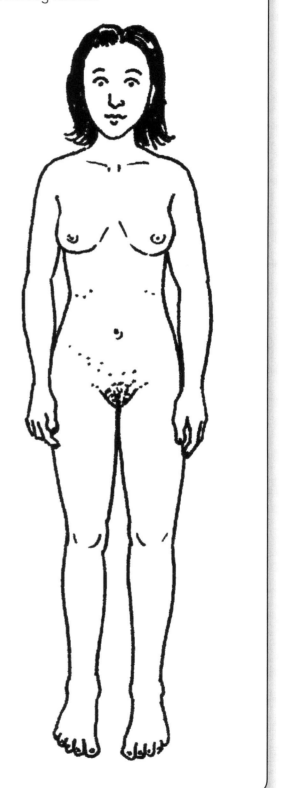

DAILY ROUTINES

19 I GET WORRIED WHEN MY TEACHER IS ABSENT

Most days we have the same teacher in my class and the same helper.

I like things to stay the same. It makes me feel OK.

But sometimes teachers are poorly. Then we have another teacher to take their place.

When this happens, we may have several teachers coming in. The other teachers share the job so that not all of the work falls on one person.

Other teachers don't know me so well. Sometimes if things go wrong, they don't know how I feel. This makes me feel upset.

These are some things I can do if I feel upset:

- Ask a friend what to do. They will share my problem.

- Ask the new teacher what to do. They will share my problem.

- Ask my helper what to do. They will share my problem.

- Go to my special place until I feel calmer.

- Write in my worry book about the thing that is upsetting me.

If I keep my problem to myself, it makes me upset.

I will try to share my problem with someone else.

Then I will feel better.

20 I KEEP FORGETTING MY BOOK BAG

Everyone in my class has a book bag.

We use it to carry books home and bring them back to school.

We also use it to carry other things, like letters, reports and school work.

When the lessons finish, we get our book bags and put books and letters and other things in them.

My teacher likes me to take my book bag home every day so that things don't get lost or spoiled.

Then my mum and dad can read the letters, read my books and help me with my work.

I will try to remember to take my book bag home every day and bring it back in the morning.

Then my mum can help me with my reading.

This will help me with my work at school.

21 CIRCLE TIME

On Thursday afternoons, I go to Circle Time.

I like Circle Time.

When I sit in the circle, I face the rest of the group. This makes my teacher happy.

I try to look at people when they are talking, to show that I am listening.

I think about other people's feelings and don't do anything to upset them.

22 I CAN GO TO SCHOOL BY MYSELF

Children go to school in various ways:

- in a car

- on a bus

- walk with mum, dad, grandparent or carer

- walk with a friend.

I walk with my mum and she takes me right into the school building.

Most children of my age come into school by themselves or with a friend.

I could find a friend who lives near me and we could walk all the way together.

This is what I will do.

- I will leave my mum outside the school grounds and go in by myself.

- I will mark the route on a map.

- Then later, I will find a friend who lives near me and we will walk all the way together, from my house.

- I will be OK.

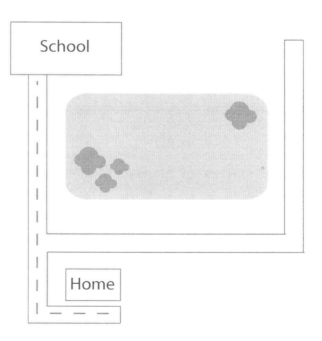

23 I CAN'T GET OUT OF BED!

Every day, children in the UK go to school.

This is because the law says they have to.

But it is also because they mostly want to.

Most of us, including me, enjoy going to school.

But I can't get out of bed!

This is because I spent quite a long time not going to school.

I got used to staying at home.

In my school planner, there are some rules that we all agree to.

I am responsible for sticking to these rules.

The rules say that I will attend school every day and arrive at the right time.

In return for this, the school will make sure that I receive a good education.

This is like an agreement between us. We both agree to do our bit.

Who is responsible? (Tick one box on the right.)

	Getting out of bed on time.	Me	☐	Parents/Carer	☐
	Getting some breakfast.	Me	☐	Parents/Carer	☐
	Getting washed and dressed.	Me	☐	Parents/Carer	☐
	Getting to the bus on time.	Me	☐	Parents/Carer	☐
	Arriving at school on time.	Me	☐	Parents/Carer	☐

Put times for each event in the boxes on the left.

I will try to stick to my agreement with school.

I will get to school on time.

24 I AM WORRIED ABOUT THE SCHOOL TOILETS

I don't like going to the school toilets.

These are some of my reasons (tick which ones apply):

- They are a long way away from the classrooms. ☐
- I don't like having to ask to go. ☐
- Sometimes bullies hang around there. ☐
- The doors don't lock properly. ☐
- Some people smoke there. ☐
- They are not supervised by adults. ☐
- They don't smell nice. ☐
- There is no toilet paper. ☐
- Some people splash water all around. ☐

Sometimes I hold on until I get home before going to the toilet.

This makes me uncomfortable all day.

What can I do to improve things?

- Find out where the toilets are nearest to my classroom. ☐
- Ask a friend to go with me or to wait nearby. ☐
- Go to the toilet in between or before lessons. ☐
- Go to the toilet before I leave home. ☐
- Take some toilet paper to school. ☐
- Report the bullies to my class teacher. ☐
- Talk or write to the school council about the smoking, the locks and the splashing. ☐
- Ask my parents to talk to the staff about some of these worries. ☐

Then I won't feel so bad.

25 SOMETIMES I FORGET TO EAT

Every day we have lunch at school.

Some people have school dinners.

Some have a lunch box.

We all have to eat our lunch in the dining room.

Some days I am busy doing things or thinking about things.

Sometimes I am not hungry at lunchtime.

I only like to eat when I feel hungry.

So, some days, at the end of lunchtime, I have not eaten anything.

Then I get hungry in the middle of the afternoon.

We are not allowed to eat during lessons.

If I am hungry then I will not be able to work properly.

I need the energy from the food to help me to work well.

I will try to remember, when the bell goes at lunchtime, I need to eat something.

I will go to the dining room and eat a bit of my lunch.

Then I will not get hungry in the afternoon.

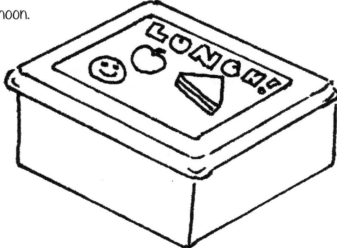

26 WHEN THE PSYCHOLOGIST COMES

Every so often in our school we have a visitor.

These are some of the sorts of people who visit my school.

1 Doctor   4 Psychologist

2 Nurse   5 Teacher of deaf children

3 School inspector   6 Teacher for autism

Any other visitors you can think of: ....

I am having a visit from a psychologist.

What will they do with me? Tick what you think.

- Tell me off.   ○
- Measure my height.   ○
- Look into my eyes.   ○
- Look at my work.   ○
- Work with me in the classroom.   ○
- Work with me outside the classroom.   ○
- Talk with me.   ○
- Shout at me.   ○
- Talk to my parents/carers.   ○
- Talk to my teacher.   ○
- Give me sweets.   ○
- Ask me to do some tests.   ○
- Make me smile.   ○
- Praise me.   ○

I will not be worried when the psychologist comes.

His/her name is ....

We will work well together. She/he will find out what I can do.

It will be enjoyable.

HOME LIFE

27 WHEN I GO TO HOLY COMMUNION

Please note: this story can be adapted for any other faith groups or religion, as appropriate.

When we go to Holy Communion, we share some bread and some wine.

We do that because Jesus did that with his followers.

When Jesus and the disciples had the Last Supper together, he said, 'Do this in remembrance of me.'

He wanted them to remember him after he was killed.

So he said of the bread, 'This is my body.'

And he said of the wine, 'This is my blood.'

When we drink the wine, we are remembering the blood of Jesus.

When we eat the bread, we are remembering the body of Jesus.

In some churches, the bread is made into little round tablets that don't look like bread.

The Bible

28 I CAN ANSWER THE PHONE

When the phone rings at my house, my mum or dad usually answers it.

I don't usually answer it. Even if the person on the phone wants to speak to me, I still don't like to do it.

If I don't answer the phone:

- the person might think there is nobody in the house
- the person might think I am rude
- my mum or dad might be embarrassed
- they might think I am not very helpful.

I will try answering the phone. This is what will happen.

- The phone rings. I pick it up and say, 'Hello. Who is it please?'
- They tell me who they are. I will remember this.
- They might ask me how I am. I will say, 'I'm fine thanks. How are you?'
- They might ask to speak to someone in my family. I will say, 'Hang on. I will go and get him/her.'
- I will put the phone down nearby.
- I will say to him/her, 'It's .... on the phone. They want to speak to you.'
- Then she/he will come to the phone and speak to the caller.

If Mum or Dad answers the phone first, the caller might ask to speak to me.

Mum or Dad will say, 'It's .... She/he would like to speak to you.'

- I will say, 'OK.' They will give me the phone. I will say, 'Hello.'
- I will listen to what they say and I will answer them.
- When I have finished, I will say, 'Bye.' Then I will ask if they want to speak to Mum or Dad again.
- If they say, 'Yes,' I will hand the phone back to Mum or Dad.
- If they say, 'No,' I will say, 'OK. Bye,' and put the phone back.

Then nobody will think I am rude. Nobody will be embarrassed.

51

29 I LIKE COLLECTING MONEY

I like collecting money.

I keep it in a special tray.

It makes me feel good to get it all out, count it and line it up.

How do I get money?

I do special jobs for my parents and they pay me.

If I find money lying around, I pick it up.

Sometimes I look in the pockets of people's clothes.

This makes them upset.

They think I am stealing.

Stealing is dishonest.

The money belongs to them and not to me.

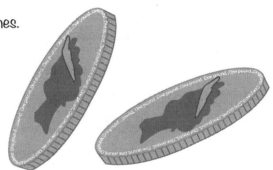

If I take money from people's pockets and other places, I will be in trouble.

I could be in trouble with the police because stealing is against the law.

I will try to stop taking money that is not mine.

I will only use money that I have earned or that someone has given me.

Then nobody will be upset.

I will not be breaking the law.

I will not be in trouble.

30 I LIKE WATCHING TELEVISION

I have a TV set in my room.

There is also one in the sitting room.

I watch some programmes in my room.

Some I watch in the sitting room.

Some I watch on my phone or tablet.

Sometimes people come to visit us.

We all sit in the sitting room.

I don't feel comfortable with lots of people in the house.

I tell them to go away when my favourite TV programme comes on.

This makes them feel unhappy.

It makes my mum unhappy.

This is what I will try to do instead.

When my favourite TV programme comes on, I will go to my room and watch it there.

Everyone else will stay in the sitting room.

They will feel comfortable with this.

My mum will feel OK about this.

I will come down again later when everyone has gone.

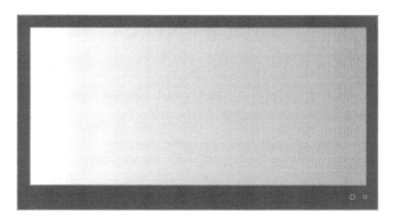

31 WHEN PEOPLE COME TO VISIT US

Friends and relatives often come to our house.

Sometimes I go to the door to let them in.

When I have let them in, I go back to my room or to what I was doing before they came.

They might think I am being rude when I do this.

It makes them feel uncomfortable.

It makes my parents feel uncomfortable too.

They like to make people feel welcome.

They want the visitors to feel as if we want them in our house.

What should I do when I meet people at the door?

- Smile.

- Say 'Hello'.

- Say, 'How are you?'

- Listen to what they say.

- If they ask how I am, I will say, 'Fine,' or I will tell them how I am.

- Go with them into the sitting room.

- Ask them if they would like a drink.

- I may help my mum to make a drink or I will stay in the sitting room and talk to them.

- If there are children with them, we may go to another room to play together.

- I will let them play with my things.

- When the people are ready to leave our house, I will come to the door and say 'Goodbye'.

If I do these things, everyone will feel welcome at our house.

SOCIAL SKILLS

32 LOOKING UP SKIRTS

Boys and men wear trousers.

Girls and women also wear trousers sometimes.

Some women wear long saris.

Some women wear short skirts and you can see their legs.

When I see a woman or a girl wearing a short skirt, I keep looking at her legs.

I want to look underneath her skirt.

Lots of boys are interested in this.

But if I wore a short skirt, I would not like people looking at my underpants!

I would be embarrassed.

When I try to look under a woman's skirt, they feel embarrassed too.

This is not a nice thing to do.

I will try to remember:

· I must not look under people's skirts.

· I will not touch them or their skirt.

Then nobody will be embarrassed.

33 THE CRAYONS BELONG TO EVERYONE

When we do colouring in our work, I like to choose some crayons to work with.

I put them on the table near my work.

Sometimes a friend might want the same colours as me.

This is OK.

But I feel annoyed if they take one of the crayons that I have chosen.

The crayons belong to all of us.

Anyone can use any colour.

My friend might say, 'Can I borrow this one?'

Then I might say, 'OK. Can I have it back afterwards please?'

Then my friend will use it and bring it back.

This is OK.

I will not get cross about it.

We can all share the crayons.

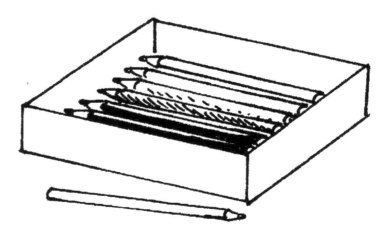

34 GO AWAY!

Sometimes when I am doing my work, I take a long time to figure things out.

People come around to try to help me and I say, 'Go away!'

I am told this sounds rude and is bad manners.

I don't like being helped because I get confused and worried, and it makes me feel embarrassed.

What can I do to make this better?

- I could use coloured cards on my desk: green = OK, red = help. Then, if they see the red card, they could help me.

- I could put my hand up and wait for someone to come and help me.

- If someone tries to help me when I don't want them to, I could say, 'I'm OK, thank you.'

- When someone has helped me, I will smile and say, 'Thank you.'

35 I KEEP TALKING

When the teacher talks to the class, I sometimes talk to my friends. This is because (tick one):

- The teacher is boring. ◯
- It doesn't matter. ◯
- I can't stop talking. ◯
- I have bad manners. ◯

This makes the teacher think (tick one):

- He is not listening. ◯
- This is really hard work. ◯
- I must be no good. ◯
- I want to tape his mouth shut. ◯
- That child has no manners. ◯

There are school rules that we are expected to agree with:

- When I speak, you listen. When you speak, I will listen.
- The teacher has a right to teach. The student has the right to learn.

If I talk all the time, the teacher can't teach and I can't learn. The other students can't learn. I am making it difficult for all of them.

I will try to remember those rules. Then I will learn.

Other students can learn.

The teacher can teach.

I will consider the teacher's feelings.

Then we will all feel better.

> Speaking and listening. When I speak, you listen. When you speak, I will listen.

59

36 I DIDN'T DO IT!

In our school, we have rules.

One of these is that we try to tell the truth.

Sometimes I do something that breaks the rules.

And sometimes I say things that upset people.

Sometimes someone sees me doing it or saying it.

If I think that I will be in trouble, I might pretend that I didn't do it or say it.

Then everyone knows I am not being truthful.

This is not OK.

If I pretend that I didn't do it or say it, I am telling a lie.

Everybody breaks the rules sometimes.

Everyone gets told off sometimes.

Then we learn not to do it next time.

I will try to tell the truth when I have done or said something wrong.

Then I won't upset anyone.

37 I DON'T LIKE BEING HELPED

Sometimes I don't understand what I have to do.

Lots of students don't understand things a lot of the time.

I don't like asking for help.

I don't like being helped.

It makes me feel different from other students.

But I am just the same as the others.

There are support assistants in most lessons.

I like some of them but not others.

Sometimes I show them I am not keen on being helped.

This makes them feel uncomfortable.

The teacher wants the assistants to help people who are having a problem.

If I don't like that person, it's not very nice for them.

I will try to ask for help when I need it by putting my hand up.

I will work with that person and say 'thank you' afterwards.

38 I GET MAD AT PEOPLE!

When we play outside, I like to have friends to play with.

We don't know who is playing with who until we get outside.

Some people play football, some baseball and some play other games, like tag or hide-and-seek.

My favourite game is ....

I like chasing and being chased.

I like catching people.

Sometimes we grab hold of each other.

Sometimes I grab a person's clothes or put my arms around them.

This often gets me into trouble because they don't like it.

They might get angry and shout at me or hit me.

Then I get angry too. Sometimes I hit them or kick them.

Then I get told off.

I have to go and calm down.

I will try not to grab people or hold them or hit them.

Then they will not get mad at me.

Then I will not get mad at them.

39 I FEEL ANGRY SOMETIMES

Some students like to make other students angry. They 'wind them up'.

People who are always getting angry get wound up a lot by other students.

Then the students have a laugh when that person gets angry.

Sometimes we tease each other for a joke.

This is normal.

When we see the joke, we can join in and laugh with them.

It can be hard to tell when a person is joking or when it is more serious.

It is even harder to ignore what they say and sometimes I want to 'get my own back'.

Some people think you should do to other people what they do to you.

'He called me a name so I called him a name.'

This might make me feel better for a while.

But it doesn't make things any better.

The same thing will happen again, later.

Here are some choices I can make. Tick one:

· Hit the person who winds me up.　　○

· Tell a teacher.　　○

· Tell a friend.　　○

· Use my 'time out' card and get out of the room.　　○

· Say nothing, do nothing.　　○

· Get very angry.　　○

· Stay calm.　　○

40 I KEEP SAYING UNKIND THINGS

One day, I said to my friend ....

....

My friend was upset.

He was upset because ....

....

When I said that, I was being unkind.

I said it without thinking about his feelings.

These are some other things that I've said that hurt people's feelings.

....

....

....

....

I will try to think about my friends' feelings.

I will try to say only kind things.

Sticks and stones may break my bones but words will wound forever.

41 I KEEP SPOILING PEOPLE'S WORK

When I am feeling cross, or I don't want to do something, sometimes I make a mark on someone else's work.

I leave my table and draw a line or scribble on a friend's book when I go by.

This might make them feel:

Happy   Sad   Angry   Upset

Then they tell the teacher and I get told off.

If somebody made a mark on my work, how would I feel?

Happy   Sad   Angry   Upset

I would not like it if someone did it to me.

I will try not to do this to my friends.

I will scribble on some scrap paper instead.

Then I will feel better.

Nobody will be upset.

42 I KEEP TELLING THEM WHAT TO DO

The other students feel annoyed if I see things clearly and they do not.

They may want to work it out for themselves.

But I am not letting them.

Me being smarter and quicker makes them feel uncomfortable.

What can I do?

Wait to see if anyone can work it out.

If they can't, say 'I think I know what to do'.

'Would you like me to show you?'

43 I KEEP THROWING THINGS

Sometimes my brain tells me to pick up something and throw it at somebody.

Sometimes it even tells me to take off my shoes or slippers and socks and throw them.

I throw them in the classroom. I throw them in assembly.

This gets people upset if they are hit by shoes or socks.

It makes them go 'Uuuuuuuurgghh!'

This is not funny. It stops the lesson.

My teacher has to stop teaching to tell me off.

It stops people from learning.

I have to be taken away to work by myself.

Why do I throw things? (Tick one.)

· I w ant to get attention.   ◯

· I don't want to do any work.   ◯

· My brain keeps telling me to do it.   ◯

How old am I? ....

How old are children who throw things? (Put a ring round the numbers.)

1   2   3   4   5   6   7   8   9   10

Does anyone else throw things in my class?   Yes   No

How old are they? ....

What should I do about it?

What should my teacher do?

I will try: ....

44 I LIKE CORRECTING PEOPLE

I always think I am right!

Sometimes I do know better than the teacher, but I must try to think of a nice way to say it, rather than a direct confrontation.

I will not say, 'See, I told you so!'

People who work in schools are there because they want to help me, not to annoy me!

I will try to think about their feelings.

45 I LIKE GETTING REWARDS

Every day we do our work.

We all try our best to do good work.

Sometimes when I do really good work, I get a sticker/stamp/point as a reward.

Sometimes my friends get rewards too.

When this happens and I don't get a reward, I get cross.

I want a reward too.

But my friends don't get cross if I get a reward.

They are pleased for me.

I will try not to get cross when someone else gets a reward and I don't.

I will smile and be pleased for my friends.

46 I LIKE TO GET MY OWN BACK

Sometimes people do things or say things to me that annoy me.

Somebody might take my pen or throw something at me.

Sometimes they might push me in the corridor or call me names.

When this happens, I want to do it back to them.

I keep on wanting to do it for a very long time.

This is called 'bearing a grudge'.

When I try to get my own back on that person, I often get into trouble.

I might be told off or get a detention, or even get into a fight.

This makes things worse. I don't feel any better.

Here are some things I can do instead:

· Ignore it. Don't react to it. Then that person might get fed up and stop doing it.

· Don't get angry. Smile and pick up the thing they threw, give it back. Carry on with my work.

· Talk to an adult about it. Let them deal with it.

· Write down my feelings in a book.

· Forget about it.

I will try not to bear grudges. Then I will feel calmer.

47 I LIKE TOUCHING PEOPLE

When I like someone very much, I like to touch them now and again. I might give my mum a hug or a kiss. Sometimes I sit very close to a friend. Sometimes I touch my teacher when I walk past her.

There are different ways to touch people.

Some touching is OK. Some touching is not OK.

It might embarrass my teacher, for instance, if I touch her bottom. Some touching is OK at home but not at school.

OK at home	OK at school	Not OK at school
Hugging	Hand holding in games or dance	Hugging
Kissing	Linking arms	Kissing
Patting	Touching in tag	Stroking
Stroking	Shaking hands	Touching bottoms
		Sitting too close
		Brushing past someone
		Hitting
		Pushing
		Kicking
		Nipping

71

48 I SAY I DIDN'T DO IT!

Sometimes I do wrong things and then deny it.

My target now is to stop denying things when I have done them.

Stopping denying things will help me to get over the problem.

If I don't deny any more, I might be the star of the day.

I might get a star on the star chart.

I might even get a sticker on my sweater.

My teacher will decide.

If I stop doing it at home as well as at school, I might get a sticker on my sticker chart, maybe two, or more!

Star of the day!

49 I SAY RUDE WORDS

At school, sometimes I say rude and silly words.

It makes me laugh but it makes my friends and teachers upset.

One of my targets is to stop saying rude and silly things.

I will try to stop doing this.

My teacher will be happy.

50 I DON'T THINK ABOUT OTHER PEOPLE'S FEELINGS

Sometimes I say things that upset my friends.

I don't always know when they are upset.

If I stop to think about other people's feelings, I might have to change the way I say some things and the way I do things.

Then I might have more friends.

51 I'M NOT SITTING WITH HER/HIM!

Sometimes we have Circle Time.

We all sit round together.

We talk about things that have happened, things that we like and things that we don't like.

We try to sort things out so that everyone will be happy.

Everyone has a say. Everyone listens.

But sometimes I don't want to join in if .... is there.

It makes me feel uncomfortable.

But if I don't join in, it isn't fair.

It makes .... feel uncomfortable.

It makes everyone feel uncomfortable.

Circle Time is a sharing time.

If I don't share, I am being selfish.

I will try to join in Circle Time.

I will sit in the circle when .... is there.

This will be fair to everyone.

52 LOOK AT ME!

When I was little, I used to call out to my mum and dad, 'Watch me do this!'

Usually they would watch me and say something good about it.

I used to like this. I kept on doing it.

When I got older, my parents got fed up with this and stopped noticing so much.

But I still liked being noticed so I used to do it to my friends.

I liked them to watch me. It made me feel good.

Now I am in secondary school.

Most of my friends have stopped doing that now.

But a few friends are still like me.

We like to get each other's attention and keep talking to each other.

This is annoying for the teachers and most of the other students.

It gets me into a lot of trouble.

The rule is that we don't talk when the teacher is talking and when we are supposed to be working.

We can talk to each other as much as we like between lessons.

I will try not to distract other pupils. I will try not to be distracted by them. Then I will not be in trouble.

53 PEOPLE SAY HORRIBLE THINGS

Sometimes I get upset at the things that people say to me.

My friend said to me ....

....

I thought my friend meant it and I felt hurt.

In school, lots of people say things that I think are unkind. These are some other things that I have heard:

....

....

....

But at school, there is a lot of jokey kind of talk.

People say things that are a bit rude but they don't mean it. It is part of the funny side of school. Things like 'You want to wash your ears out!'

I find it hard to understand this.

But I will try to smile next time someone says anything like that to me.

Then they will know that I am OK.

I will try not to get upset.

54 I DON'T LIKE THEM WINDING ME UP

Winding people up is a normal thing for people to do.

It is a way of having fun with each other.

Most people get the joke and have a laugh about it.

I find this hard to do.

What can I do? (Tick one.)

- Get angry and shout at them. ◯

- Run away. ◯

- Tell them I don't get it. ◯

- Ignore them. ◯

I will try to look at their face to see whether they are being serious or funny.

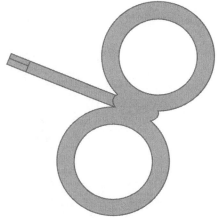

55 I LIKE PLAY FIGHTING

I like watching fights on TV and in films.

My favourite programmes or films are ....

My favourite characters are ....

I try to copy what they do with my friends at school.

This is called 'play fighting'.

Sometimes when I play fight, my friends get hurt.

Then I get into trouble.

When people fight on TV, or in a film, it looks real but it is only pretending. Nobody really gets hurt.

When I am play fighting, I will try to remember it is only pretend fighting. I won't hit or kick anyone.

Then nobody will be hurt and I won't be in trouble.

56 GAMES IN THE PLAYGROUND

My friends say I keep wanting to join in their games but then I spoil the game, start sulking and get cross.

I go to tell a teacher. She talks to them about it but, afterwards, they still say I can't play because I am moody.

But they don't tell me the rules.

They keep changing them so I don't understand.

If they don't tell me what is going on, I find it hard to know what to do.

My choices are (choose the best one):

- Talk to some friends before going out to play. ○
- Ask what they are playing and whether I can join them. ○
- If I don't understand a new rule, don't get mad. ○
- Stop and ask someone what is going on. ○

57 I GET CROSS IF THINGS DON'T GO MY WAY

I wanted to play cricket at lunchtime, but the others got there first.

I had cricket in my head, but no one else knew this.

I have to tell someone.

If there is a cricket rota, I will get my name on it.

Then I will know when it is my turn to play.

I could also ask a friend, 'Can I play cricket with you?'

58 SIR/MISS, YOU'VE MADE A MISTAKE!

Sometimes my teacher spells something wrong on the board. I like telling my teacher off. I say, 'You've spelt that wrong. Are you thick or something?'

Then the teacher gets mad and sends me out. Then I get mad. It's boring out there with nothing to do.

What could I do to make this better?

If I notice a spelling mistake, I could:

- put up my hand and wait

- ask the teacher if he/she will come and have a word with me

- ask quietly how to spell the word and say, 'Is that how you spelled it on the board?'

Then, when the teacher sees the mistake, he/she will thank me for pointing it out.

If I tell off the teacher so everyone can hear, the teacher will be embarrassed.

If we discuss it together quietly, the teacher will feel better and I won't be sent out.

59 SOME PEOPLE LOOK A BIT DIFFERENT

My friend has big ears. One day, I told him what big ears he has. He got very upset and was in tears.

Some people have things that are different from most children.

Here are some examples. Can you think of a few more?

· Big ears

· Unusual hair

· Very fat

People like this know they are different. They can be upset when somebody tells them about it. They know they can't change the way they are.

When I see somebody who is different like this, I can look but I will not say anything. If I tell them about it, they might get upset.

I will try not to upset people. I will talk about something else.

60 PEOPLE WHO ARE DIFFERENT

Some people have skin that is a different colour to mine.

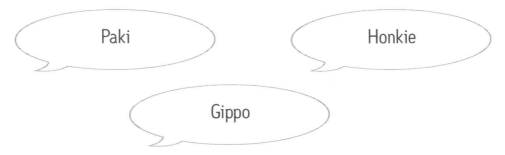

Paki

Honkie

Gippo

Some people don't like people who are different from themselves.

They call them names, such as 'nigger' and 'chocolate' and 'white trash' or 'Paki'.

In my school, there are people from different backgrounds, such as Pakistani, English and African-Caribbean families.

Everyone is welcome in my school.

It doesn't matter what they look like or where they come from.

We are all equal.

We all learn together.

We learn about each other.

If someone gets called an unpleasant name, it makes them feel very unhappy.

It can also make them angry.

I will try not to call them unpleasant names when I see someone who is different from me.

I will call them by their first name.

61 WALKING ON THE PAVEMENT

When we go out walking, we walk on the pavement.

We walk on the pavement because it is safe.

Cars go on the road. People go on the pavement.

On the pavement we won't get knocked down by a car.

The kerb is on the edge of the pavement. It divides the road from the pavement.

If I walk on the kerb, some of me sticks out into the road. I might get hit by a car or a truck.

I will try to walk on the pavement and not on the kerb.

Then I will not get hit by a car or a truck.

I will be safe.

62 I DON'T LIKE IT WHEN PEOPLE SHOUT

Sometimes someone in my class does something bad. My teacher gets annoyed and might shout at them. Sometimes the children shout at each other.

This upsets me and I feel like crying.

Whose problem is it? (Underline one.)

Mine   The other child

Who sorts it out? (Underline one.)

Me   My teacher

Who needs to worry about it? (Underline one.)

Me   The other child   My teacher

I don't need to get upset because it is not my fault.

I don't have to deal with it. It is someone else's problem.

I will try to ignore it when someone shouts. I can put my hands over my ears. I will not cry. I will get on with my work.

63 I GET UPSET WHEN THERE IS A LOT OF NOISE

When the children are coming in from break and the teacher is not in charge, I find it hard to handle the noise they make and the silly behaviour.

> Autism says, 'Shut up you lot or I will tell the teacher. Someone might get hurt.' Autism likes to be bossy!

In art lessons, the children are more noisy than in, say, a maths lesson.

This is because people like to chat while they are doing things with their hands, or something which is fun.

So the teacher lets them talk more. I find this hard to handle.

My choices are (choose the best one):

· Tell them off.

· Join in with the naughty behaviour.

· Get on with my work and try to ignore them.

· Ask if I can do my artwork in a quieter place, perhaps with a friend.

64 WHY ARE THEY LAUGHING AT ME?

Sometimes when I say things, I notice that other children laugh or smile.

When I notice people laughing, I think they are laughing at me.

At other times, I notice people talking together and I think they are talking about me.

When this happens, I get upset.

Maybe I think too much about myself.

Maybe when they smile it is because they like me.

Perhaps when they laugh they are laughing about something else.

There are lots of things that make people laugh.

There are lots of things to talk about besides me.

Maybe I could go to them and say, 'What are you talking about?'

I could ask them what they are laughing about.

They might share it with me.

If I do this then I might not feel so upset.

65 BODY LANGUAGE

Positives

- Smile.

- Look at the person.

- Face my body towards them.

- Don't fold my arms.

- Use 'open' gestures.

- Stop what I am doing.

- Give the person my full attention.

- Use a light, friendly tone of voice.

Negatives

- Not smiling.

- Not looking at them.

- Arms folded.

- 'Closed' gestures.

- Carrying on working.

- Not giving them attention.

- Heavy or uninterested tone of voice.

89

66 WHY DO I HAVE TO LOOK AT PEOPLE?

Sometimes when a person speaks to me, I don't want to listen to them.

So I turn my back on them.

It makes me feel uncomfortable when a person looks into my eyes.

Most people look into each other's eyes when they are talking to each other. But I can listen without looking into a person's eyes.

Most teachers like to look at a student's face when they speak to them. This makes them feel sure that the student is listening.

If the student does not look at them, they think they are not listening. If I turn my back on a teacher, they will think this is rude. Then I will get into trouble.

When a teacher or another adult talks to me, I will remember not to turn my back on them.

I will try to look at them some of the time, then they will know I am listening.

I won't get into trouble.

67 GREETING PEOPLE

I don't want to smile if I don't feel like it.

People think I am unfriendly.

It looks as if I am not interested in them.

Smiling is catching. Most people do it.

A smile says, 'I like you.'

Even if I don't like someone, it is good to smile back.

It makes a person feel valued.

68 WHY DO I WHISPER?

Sometimes I whisper when I am talking to my friends.

I do this because I think it is fun.

My friends don't think it is fun.

They can't understand what I am saying!

This is not OK.

I will try to think about their feelings.

I will remember not to whisper.

69 WHY DON'T THEY STICK TO THE RULES?

When we have games run by the teacher, everyone sticks to the rules.

If they don't, they might get sent off.

I like it when people stick to the rules. It makes it fair.

When we play games in the playground, we don't have a teacher in charge.

The children sometimes make up their own rules. Sometimes they break the rules.

I don't like it when they change the rules. It makes me feel uncomfortable and sometimes angry.

Sometimes I leave the game.

What can I do about it? Choose the best ones.

- Stay calm. Stay in the game.

- Get angry. Leave the game.

- Come back later when I have calmed down.

- Tell a teacher.

- Talk to the children who broke the rules.

- Sort out the rules before we start.

- Play something else.

70 YOU'VE MADE A MISTAKE!

Sometimes when we are working, I see that a friend has made a mistake.

Sometimes I hear them giving the wrong answer.

When this happens, I want to tell them about it so they will know it is wrong.

If I do this, they might get upset.

It makes them feel bad when a friend tells them off.

Tick whose job it is to tell children about their mistakes:

Mine ◯

Teacher's ◯

When we make a mistake, we learn to do it right the next time.

I will try not to tell off my friends when they get things wrong.

I will let the teacher do that.

Then they will not be upset.

HOMEWORK

71 I DON'T WANT TO DO SCHOOL WORK AT HOME

Every day we do work at school. Sometimes we don't finish all the work in the lessons.

Our teacher wants us to finish the work at home.

Sometimes they set extra work to do at home.

These are usually bits of work where we have to practise a bit more, or find out something, or go on the internet.

There isn't time to do this in the lessons.

Our school has an agreement with the parents or carers and the students.

The school agreement

- The teachers agree to teach us.

- The parents and carers agree to support them.

- They also agree to help us with homework.

- The students agree to do the work in school and at home.

Every school has an agreement like this.

The reason I am allowed to go to this school is that I have agreed to do these things. Did I know that?

Maybe I should ask to see a copy of this agreement.

Then I will know what I am expected to do.

Then I will feel happier about doing the homework.

72 HELP! I CAN'T DO MY HOMEWORK!

Sometimes when I get home, I look in my planner or in my work book and I can't remember what I have to do or I don't understand the work.

Even when I ask my mum or dad, they don't understand it either.

Then I get upset or worried in case I get in trouble with the teacher.

Why does this happen?

· Because I didn't understand the work in the lesson.

· I didn't have time to write it down.

· I was afraid to ask for help.

What can I do to make it better?

· Ask the teacher to explain it to me.

· Ask my support assistant to help.

· Ask my support assistant to write it down in my work book.

· If I can't do it at home, I will stop and put it aside. Then I can go to my support assistant or teacher the next day and ask for help.

· I can say, 'Sorry I didn't understand it', or 'I forgot what to do, can you help me please?'

· They won't be cross with me. They will be glad that I asked for help. They will give me more time.

· It will be OK.

73 WHAT HAPPENS IF I CAN'T DO MY HOMEWORK?

Some days I have to take work home from school.

Sometimes I can't remember what to do.

And sometimes the work is too hard.

Even my mum or dad can't help me.

I get worried when I can't do it.

I think I will be in trouble at school.

Everyone has difficulty at times with their work.

This is quite normal.

My teacher will not be angry with me.

This is what I have to do.

- I will make sure I have clear instructions in my book/planner before I take it home.

- I will try hard to do my work.

- If I can't do it, I will ask Mum or Dad to help.

- If they can't help me, I will stay calm.

- I will stop working and put it away.

- I will ask Mum or Dad to write a note to my teacher.

- I will take the note to my teacher.

- I will ask for some more help.

- Then I will try again.

It will be OK.

74 WHAT HAPPENS IF I MISS SOME HOMEWORK?

Sometimes I am not in school on the day that homework is set.

I might be ill or have a hospital appointment.

I don't know what work I have to do.

I won't be able to hand in my work to the teacher.

I get worried when this happens.

I think I might be punished for not doing the work.

What can I do?

- I can tell the teacher when I get back that I was ill and I missed the homework.

- I can ask if he/she will explain what work I have to do.

What will the teacher do?

- He/she might give me extra time to do the work.

- He/she might say I don't have to do it.

I will not be punished if I tell the teacher.

It will be OK.

81 I CAN'T GET STARTED

In every lesson, the teacher starts off by talking to us about the work we have to do.

I listen but often I don't take in everything the teacher says.

Then we have to start doing our work.

Usually, one of the support assistants comes round to ask me if I know what I have to do.

I usually do know what to do but being asked makes me feel better.

Then I can get started.

But my teacher wants me to get started on my own.

Everyone else gets started on their own.

If I sit and wait for someone to help me, I am wasting working time.

The teacher and the support assistant go round and help other children while they are working.

Even if they get something wrong, it doesn't matter because the teacher will help them to get it right.

Nobody is in trouble for getting things wrong.

I will remember this the next time I have to start working.

I will start working by myself, then I will not be wasting time.

I will not wait for someone to come and tell me.

I will not get into trouble if I get it wrong.

It will be OK.

Nobody is in trouble for getting things wrong.

82 I GET DISTRACTED

When I work on my own, I find it hard to keep working.

If someone is talking over there, I want to join in.

If someone is sharpening a pencil, I like to watch them.

I might see something interesting out of the window.

So I don't get any work done.

What happens if I don't do any work?

- I get told off.

- I learn nothing.

- I have to lose some of my playtime.

What will help me to work on my own?

- I can have a separate desk in a corner.

- I can use a timer.

- I can have a sign saying, 'I am working independently'.

- I can keep my eyes on my work.

Which one would I like best?

I will ....

> **I am working independently.**

83 STAYING ON TASK

This is a teacher's way of saying 'getting on with your work'.

It is hard to ignore other people talking nearby.

I think they are talking about me.

Usually they are not.

I will try to ignore them and get on with my work.

Keep your 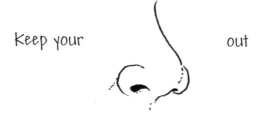 out

I am thinking my own thoughts while the teacher is talking.

Lots of people with autism do that.

But so do hundreds of people without autism.

It is the teacher's job to do something about it.

If I don't know what to do when the work starts, I will ask a friend.

84 I GET WORRIED IF I DON'T FINISH ON TIME

When I am working, it takes me a long time to work out what I have to do.

It takes me a long time to write things down.

I need more time than other people.

When the end of the lesson gets near, I get worried because I haven't finished the work.

I will try to remember:

· Lots of other students don't finish the work.

· The teacher won't be cross with me.

· I will not get a detention.

· I can finish the work for homework.

· I can finish it in the next lesson.

· I can ask an adult to write in my book any bits that I have missed.

· I can ask a friend to help me to do this.

· I can tell the teacher that I have not finished.

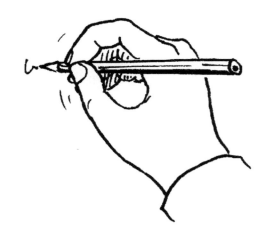

It will be OK!

85 TEACHERS DON'T LISTEN TO ME

I am never asked for my opinion. Why is this?

My opinion is very important. Everyone must hear it.

How many people are there in my class?

How long would it take for the teacher to hear all of them?

Maybe she knows that I always have the answer, so she doesn't need to worry about me.

Maybe she wants other people to have a chance to think about it.

Maybe she wants to let people hear others getting it wrong so the rest won't feel so bad about it.

I will think about this.

If I always know the answer, it might make other people feel stupid.

86 I DON'T UNDERSTAND!

I keep putting my hand up but the teacher ignores me.

Maybe he thinks that I have all the answers or that I put my hand up too much.

I will go to the teacher later on and quietly say, 'I didn't understand that. Could you help me please?'

87 I KEEP GETTING DETENTIONS

Sometimes when I have broken a school rule, I get put in detention. This means that I will have to give up some of my playtime or time after school.

I might get a detention because:

- I didn't hand in my homework on time.

- I misbehaved in a lesson.

- I didn't do enough work in the lesson.

- (other reason) ....

In detention, sometimes we have to do some more work or the teacher tells us off, or we just sit quietly.

I won't come to any harm in detention.

I will only lose a bit of free time.

I can avoid getting detention if:

- I do all my work.

- I hand in my homework on time.

- I ask for help when I need it.

- I don't fool around.

88 I LIKE DRAWING ON MY WORK

When I am doing my work, sometimes I do little drawings in my book.

It makes me feel calm and happy.

This makes my teacher get cross with me.

She/he says it spoils my work.

Teachers like us to do writing in writing books and maths in maths books.

Sometimes we do diagrams.

Sometimes we do pictures if it belongs to the work.

But we don't do drawing unless the teacher tells us to.

If I have a drawing book with me, I could draw in that.

Each time I finish a piece of work in numeracy or literacy, or other subjects, I could spend a few minutes doing drawings in my drawing book.

Then I will feel OK.

My teacher won't be cross.

89 I LIKE TO DO PERFECT WRITING

When I am doing my work, it takes me a long time to write words.

I like it to look really smart and I don't like to make any mistakes.

This means I work slower than other children.

Usually I don't finish the work.

So when I need to look at it again, some of the information is missing.

How can I get all the work done?

1   I can practise writing faster.

2   I can stop worrying about making mistakes.

3   I could do some of the writing on the computer.

4   I could ask an adult to write what I want to say.

5   If I do a bit of it first, an adult could finish it off.

If I do 3, 4 or 5, my teacher can see
what I have learned, even though I didn't
do all of the writing with my pen.

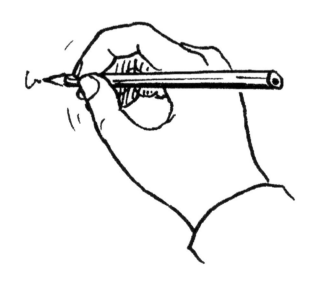

It will look good.

I will finish the work.

It will be OK.

89 I LIKE TO DO PERFECT WRITING

90 I WANT ONE TOO!

I like to get rewards such as stickers or house points.

I do good work every day and I would like to get a reward every day.

One day, my friend got a reward for doing some good work.

I got cross because I didn't get one.

My teacher said this was not fair.

Everybody gets rewards from time to time.

But nobody gets rewards every day.

If we did then rewards would not be so special.

Well Done!

I will try to do good work every day.

But when somebody else gets a reward, I will try not to get cross.

I will be happy for them.

I will say, 'Well done. You did some good work.'

91 IT'S OK TO BE DIFFERENT

Every student in school is different.

Some are short and some are tall.

Some have fair hair and some have dark hair.

Some can't hear as well as others.

Some can't see small print and some can.

It's OK to be different.

We all have a right to be here together.

I find it hard to read small print or writing on the board.

Sometimes this makes it hard for me to do my work.

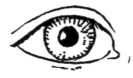 

This is how the school helps me:

· I have copies of my work in large print.

· I can go up to the board for a closer look.

· I can put up my hand to ask for help.

It's OK to have the same work as other students in large print. Then I can read it better.

It's OK to ask for help. Everyone asks for help when they need it.

I will try to ask for help when I need it.

92 TESTS!

Everyone in my school has to do tests.

They help the teachers to see how well we have learned our work.

I don't like doing tests. I get worried about them.

My teacher says it doesn't matter how many tests I get right or wrong, just as long as I have a go.

I will have a go and try my best, then I might not get worried.

Have a go and try your best.

93 WE WORK IN A GROUP

When we sit at the table together, we are working in a group.

When our teacher is talking, we look at her/him.

We don't talk.

We listen to her/him.

This is good listening and good looking.

When we do our work, we sit up straight.

We stay at the table until we have finished.

We don't touch anyone.

This is good working.

94 TAKING TURNS

When I am working in a group, I want to have things my way and I want the others to hurry up.

This annoys them.

Sometimes the work ends before I have had a turn.

This annoys me.

I like to be in control.

My choices are (choose the best one):

- Get mad and sulk.

- Ask if I can have a turn next time.

- Stay cool. It doesn't matter.

95 WHAT TO DO WHEN I HAVE FINISHED MY WORK

Choose the most useful answers below and underline them.

Draw suitable pictures in the boxes.

Go to sleep.

Read a book.

Annoy my neighbour.

Tell the teacher.

Check for mistakes. Make some corrections.

Help someone else to finish their work.

Go home.

96 WHY DO I HAVE TO DO WRITING?

Every day I do my work in school and I learn new things.

My teacher always makes us write down what we have learned.

I don't like writing.

When I have learned something, I keep it in my head.

Why do I have to write so many things?

Teachers like me to write things down because it helps me to remember it better. And they can see what I have done. And my parents can too.

Also, I can look at it later when I need to get ready for a test.

If it is only in my head, how will my teacher know that I have learned it?

I will remember when I don't want to do writing, why I have to do it.

Writing is part of the work.

Then my teacher and my mum and dad will be pleased.

97 WHY DO I HAVE TO PRACTISE?

Every week I have a keyboard lesson.

My teacher gives me pieces of music to play.

Sometimes it is hard to play and she/he wants me to do it lots of times.

Usually there is not enough time to finish it.

She/he will ask me to practise it.

This means do it again and again until I get it right.

Sometimes there is not time to practise at school.

I have to practise at home.

If I practise it, I will play better.

If my playing gets better, my teacher will be pleased.

She/he can give me better pieces of music to play.

I will try to practise every day at home.

I will do it again and again until I get it right.

Then I will get better pieces of music to play.

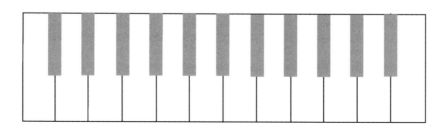

98 WHY DO WE DO THINGS TWICE?

Every day we do writing. Sometimes we have to do things twice.

My teacher says we have to do a first draft and then a best copy.

When I have done my first draft, all of my thoughts have come out and I feel as if I have finished. I don't want to do it again.

But my teacher says the first draft is important but if anyone read it, they would have difficulty.

There are often spelling mistakes. There are crossings out.

The ideas are sometimes in the wrong order. Sometimes things are repeated and sometimes things are left out.

It needs to be smartened up and better organised.

The second draft has to look better with no spelling mistakes or crossings out. Then it will be easier to read.

Next time I do some writing, I will think about the reader.

I will correct all of my spellings from the first draft and there will be no crossing out.

It will be better organised.

The second draft will look good and be easy to read.

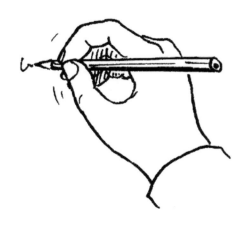

99 YOU CAN DO BETTER THAN THAT!

When I am doing my work, I don't like anyone watching me.

When I have finished, I will show it to ....

Sometimes they tell me I have to change things to make them better. I don't like this. I sometimes get mad.

Usually when a teacher or a support assistant tells me this, it is because they know I have done it too quickly and, if I took more time, I could do it better.

I will try not to get mad when I am asked to do it again.

I will try to do it more carefully to start with.

But I will do it again and try to make it better.

Then .... will be pleased with me.

100 PROBLEMS

This is a word that causes me problems!

The problem is that it is a normal sort of word and I hear people saying it a lot, maybe in a way which makes it sound like an insult.

'You've got problems!'

Everyone has problems.

It is normal to have problems.

> I hate maths.
>
> I hate football.
>
> I keep getting angry.

Teachers have problems! (Like children – joke!)

What can I do to sort out problems?

I can go to a teacher and say, 'I've got a problem. Can you help me please?'

I can go to a friend and ask the same question.

Most teachers or friends will be happy to help me.

They like being asked.

It makes them feel good if I think they can help with a problem.

PLAYTIME, PE AND GAMES

101 FINDING A FRIEND

Sometimes when I go out to play, I have no one to play with.

I follow .... around because I want to play with him.

But .... sometimes wants to play with someone else.

If I follow him around, he might be annoyed.

He might say to me, 'Go and play with someone else.'

If he says that, I won't follow him any more.

I will try to find someone else to play with.

I will ask somebody, 'Could I play with you please?'

Then .... will feel better.

And I will feel better.

102 I CAN SWIM IN DEEPER WATER

When we go to swimming lessons, we usually wear arm bands.

Sometimes we also hold on to things that float.

These things help us to swim without sinking.

I can swim without putting my feet down.

But I like to swim in shallow water so that I can put my feet down on the bottom if I want to.

Sometimes the teacher asks us to swim in deeper water. Then I don't feel so safe.

But the teacher knows that I will be all right with my arm bands and floats.

They will not ask me to do anything they know I can't do.

So maybe I will trust the teacher when he/she asks me to swim in deep water.

I will not panic or get upset.

I will be OK!

103 WE HAVE SWIMMING LESSONS

Every week we go to the swimming pool.

We learn how to swim because we need to be safe in the water.

If I fell in the river, I would be OK if I could swim.

We wear arm bands and floats.

These keep us from sinking under the water.

We all have fun in the swimming pool.

One day I will take my feet off the bottom and just float.

This will be fun.

I will be OK.

104 WHEN I PLAY POOL

What skills do I need?

- Taking aim with the cue.

- Potting the ball.

- Taking turns.

- Waiting patiently when it is not my turn.

- Watching my partner when it is their turn.

- Saying something nice when they score, like 'Well done' or 'Nice one'.

- Staying cool if they win and I lose.

- Saying 'Thank you' to my partner.

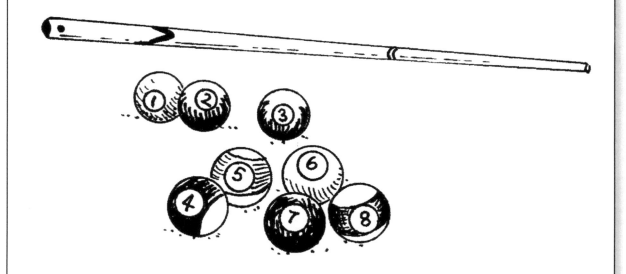

105 WHY DO I HAVE TO GET CHANGED?

There are special clothes for different activities.

Cyclists wear tight-fitting clothes to cut down wind resistance.

We put on a coat when it rains to keep warm and dry.

We wear an apron or an old shirt when we do painting.

When we do PE and games, we change our clothes.

We need loose clothing that allows our limbs to move freely.

We wear shorts to allow us to stretch our legs.

We wear T-shirts or vests so that we can stretch our arms.

We wear pumps or trainers so that our feet won't slip.

They are light so that we can move fast.

We wear these clothes so that everyone can look the same.

I would look silly if I wore my everyday clothes for PE.

I will get changed at the same time as everyone else.

Then we can all do PE together.

106 WHY THE SWIMMING TEACHER HAS TO SHOUT

When we go to swimming lessons, we have a different teacher.

This teacher has lots of classes from different schools.

So this teacher doesn't know me like my class teacher does.

The swimming pool is a big, noisy, echoey place.

Sometimes our ears are under the water.

It is hard for the teacher to talk to all of the children.

So she has to shout a lot to be heard.

I don't like it when teachers shout. It upsets me.

But if the teacher didn't shout, I wouldn't be able to hear.

I will try to remember that the teacher is not cross with me when she/he shouts.

That is what they have to do in the swimming pool.

I will try to listen to what the teacher says and do what I am asked.

I won't be upset.

PART 2
CARTOONS AND OTHER VISUAL TECHNIQUES

CONTENTS

C1 ANGER

1 Getting things wrong, for example, maths.

2 Being wound up.

C2 GETTING INTO GROUPS

C3 GOOD MANNERS

Which way is best?

C4 I WANT TO TAKE PENALTIES

We go out to play football.

I like it when I get to kick.

I like taking penalties.

The others don't like it when I stop the game to take penalties. This is not fair on them.

This makes me cross.

When I have to leave the game, I get angry.

I will try to be fair.

I won't stop the game, I will stay calm.

C5 WHAT TO DO WHEN A TEACHER IS CROSS

Tick:

☐ Worry   ☐ Cry   ☐ Ignore   ☐ Put hands over ears

Tick:

☐ Cry   ☐ Kick door   ☐ Say sorry   ☐ Ask for help

C6 WORKING IN A GROUP

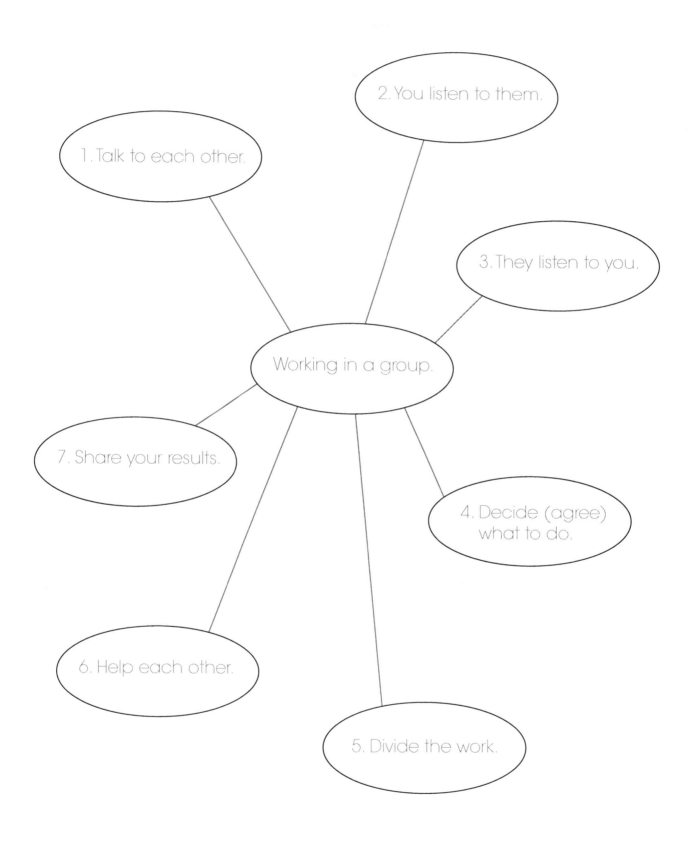

C7 WHY IT IS BEST NOT TO INSULT OTHER CHILDREN OR THEIR FAMILIES

Two boys are fighting in the playground.

The teacher is very, very angry.

One of the boys has been using insulting language.

Both of the boys were punished for fighting, but the head teacher also sent a letter to Billy's parents.

When she read the letter Billy's mum was very unhappy.

Billy's mum made Billy promise not to insult other people because it is never funny.

When Billy had stopped saying rude things to other people, playtimes became great fun. Everyone was much happier... Especially Billy.

C8 HOMEWORK

Many of the students are logical thinkers. This way of looking at a situation takes out the emotional aspects and gives the students a routine to follow.

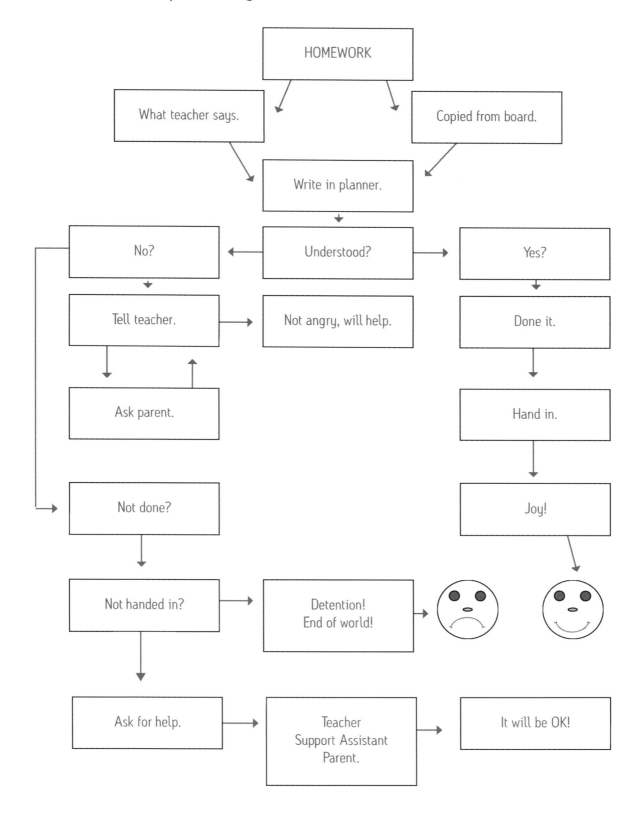

C9 ASPERGER SYNDROME MEANS ...

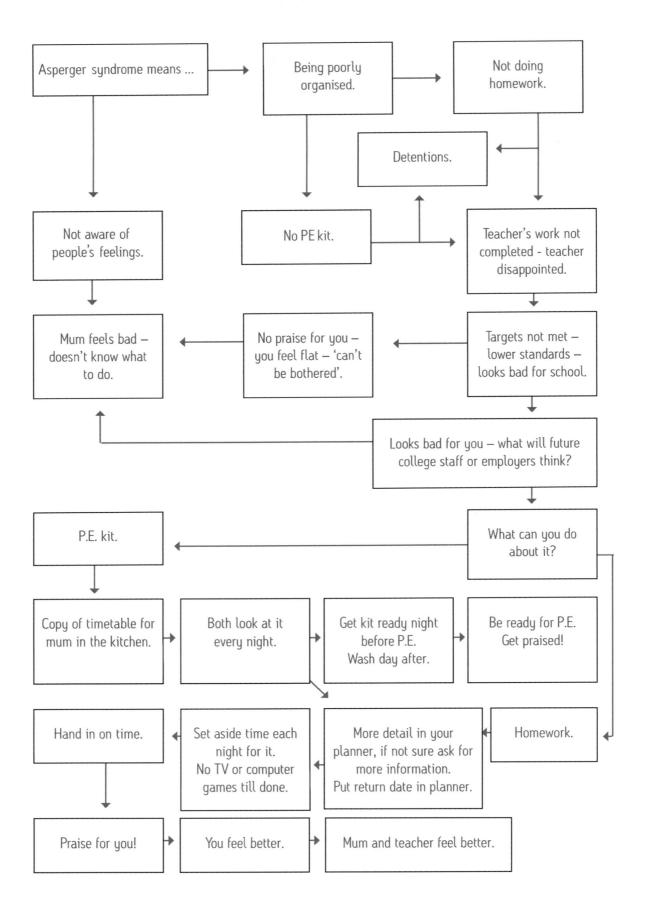

PART 3
CONTEXT

SETTING THE CONTENTS IN A REAL CONTEXT

An angry father grumbles at the teacher who has just sent his son home because of some outrageous behaviour: 'He can't help it, you know. It's his condition!' A support worker was heard saying to other children in the playground, 'Leave him alone. He can't help it.' Teenagers often make that gesture of twisting one finger against their temple – a universal symbol meaning 'not right in the head'.

Well, they are all wrong. The child can help it. The father can help it. And all the other children can help it too. But they all need help to do it. This book is about how you can do that.

We all live inside a story

Inside that story we all play out a role. That role is sometimes created for us by other people and sometimes it is created by us for our survival. We are the angry brother, or the spoilt sister, or the strong disciplinarian father, or the class clown, or perhaps the loner, the outsider. For example, one boy told me, 'Everybody knows I've got a short fuse, so they keep out of my way.' He knew his role. They knew theirs!

It is difficult for us to break out of that role – to go against type – because everyone expects us either to be what they have taught us to be or to stay where they have put us. So, for example, if father and son have become habituated to a life of conflict, it is hard for either of them to be anything else in each other's presence. If a pattern of behaviour has become fixed – such as bully and victim in school – the bullies cannot lose face by adopting a different posture. And the victim finds it impossible to be seen to be anything else.

The power of story

Story is possibly the most effective medium for learning and teaching. Who could easily forget the message of an Aesop fable or a Bible story? Many of the great religious figures in history used story as a teaching method. We can all recognise ourselves in a story and empathise with the characters. Why else are the television 'soaps' so popular?

So, by turning a child's, or a group of children's, behaviour into a narrative in which they read about themselves, we can help them to:

- remember what we have talked about

- get the point of it

- give it due consideration

- move towards changing things that are not right

- add new responses that will help to make things right.

Many of the stories in this book began as dialogues with school classes, with families and with individual children. They were written down as a record and turned into booklets or posters which the children could read again and again, as they might a record of the latest school trip.

The stories worked best when we had a diligent teacher or assistant, or parent, who helped the child or the class to revisit the stories when the need arose and even added more stories to the collection.

From the years I worked in Kirklees with children with autism, Asperger syndrome and other related conditions, I believe that the children needed to learn about themselves and how others see them and that, by the time they leave school, they should be able to explain to a potential employer what their strengths and difficulties are. 'If you can't explain your problems to yourself, how can you explain your problem to others?' (Gerland, 2000).

This applied not just to children with a diagnosis of a recognised condition. Young people whose condition is similar – what might be called 'near-miss diagnoses' – have just as much need to understand themselves, and for others to understand them, as those who do get diagnosed. We began to realise that there were numerous children out there who are, to all intents and purposes, 'on the spectrum', who were undiagnosed and not getting much help either in school or at home. So we extended our service to embrace short interventions for the more needy cases.

There are various services which try to help children and their parents and carers to cope with erratic and sometimes violent behaviour. But these services are often clinic-based and time-limited. The demand is high and supply is limited. Families who are told about a new diagnosis and those who do not get one need, above all, time. Time to take in the meaning of what they are told, time to reassess what they already do or don't do for the child. Or simply time to think about it and read about it.

They often need many repetitions before they even understand it. And then, as the child grows and changes, they need more help to deal with evolving behaviour as it occurs over the years. Neither the child nor the parents, the peer group and family or the teacher can learn all they need to know about their child's condition and behaviour in the short time allowed in a clinical consultation or a brief period of training, if they get any (see Newson, 2000).

They need sensitive and careful counselling over a number of weeks, and in some cases, over a longer period as they come to terms with the diagnosis and its implications.

(Jones, 2001)

I would add that young people who have no diagnosis, but similar behaviours, have an even harder time in understanding themselves and in being understood by their teachers and peers.

It has been my role over the past few years to give time to these children. To listen to them, to level with them and to help them to work out for themselves different ways to behave. It seems to me that the need for this doesn't end. We have gone on to extend this to young adults after school and to encourage staff in further education to include this kind of counselling in their work.

INVOLVING THE OTHER CHILDREN

This book also includes the rest of the children in the class, the year group and, in a few cases, the entire school, as well as the family. A child cannot help himself alone. Any intervention has to include those around him. I think that the responsibility for changing behaviour is a shared responsibility between the child and his peers, teachers and family. They all have to change their role in the story.

Helping the other children to understand

The children this book is written for are often seen as very different by the other children in their class and in the rest of the school or neighbourhood. There is a very strong herd instinct to be just like everyone else. Children who do not share this are instinctively perceived as 'other'. For many, this leads to teasing and bullying. The majority of children are very tolerant and care for the 'oddballs' among them but they often don't know what to do to include the child. So they take the path of least resistance and unknowingly exclude him. The alternative requires a bit of an effort. As adults, we often do this too.

A child who is 'different' does not know what to do or say to become included and accepted socially. I challenge the rest of the class to take this on board and I wish that every school would make this part of the hidden curriculum. Saying 'He can't help it' is not good enough. They can help it with a little help from their friends and family.

Once the children understand why the 'different' child does what he does, and know how difficult it is for him to be 'normal', they are invariably kind and thoughtful about it. Bullying diminishes, excluding behaviour reduces, and the stress on the child is lessened.

Even so, as I work with the child and the children around him, my time with them is only brief compared with time spent with their teacher and other staff members. We hope to be helped by the staff in the school and the family. The ideas in this book, and the information the child has to come to terms with, need a lot of repetition. One reading and then putting it away in a folder is not enough. One boy was so put out by the challenges he was given that he used to screw up my notes and throw them away! So I sent extra copies for his parents and teachers to read with him.

Where the person's initial response was anger, this does not necessarily indicate that it was wrong to introduce him to his or her diagnosis. The first discussion is but the start of an ongoing process of gradually explaining the underlying reasons for their behaviour, difficulties and strengths. The explanations can be frequently returned to when opportunities present themselves.

(Jones, 2001)

Airborne

☐ **1** **Gyrating gyroplanes**

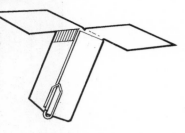

☐ **9** Make a collection of seeds. Find out which travels the furthest

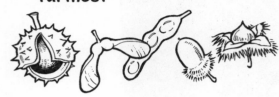

☐ **2** **Bouncing conkers**

☐ **3** **Make a super-parachute**

☐ **8** Find a way to send a 20 gram load 6 metres using air

Airborne

☐ **7** Make a Warmaline plane to travel 5 metres

☐ **4** **Magnificent paper planes**

☐ **6** **Incredible balloon rockets**

☐ **5** **Moving air**

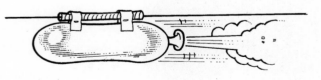

NAME:

Cross-curricular links

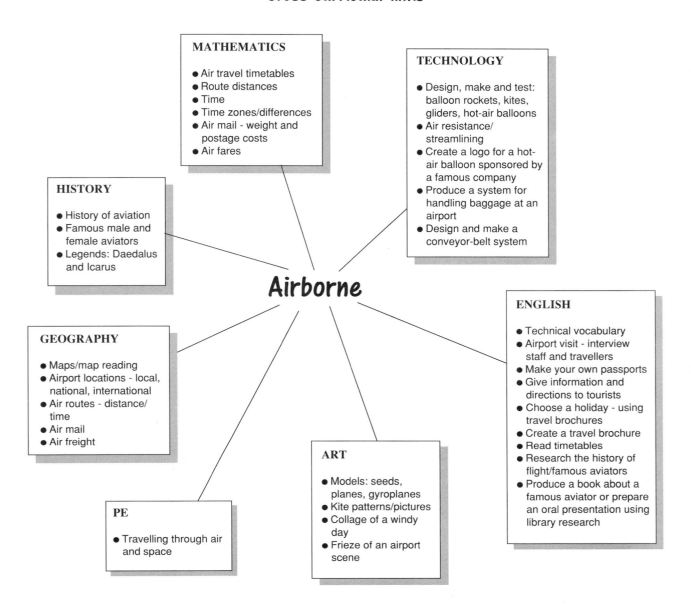

MATHEMATICS

- Air travel timetables
- Route distances
- Time
- Time zones/differences
- Air mail - weight and postage costs
- Air fares

TECHNOLOGY

- Design, make and test: balloon rockets, kites, gliders, hot-air balloons
- Air resistance/ streamlining
- Create a logo for a hot-air balloon sponsored by a famous company
- Produce a system for handling baggage at an airport
- Design and make a conveyor-belt system

HISTORY

- History of aviation
- Famous male and female aviators
- Legends: Daedalus and Icarus

Airborne

ENGLISH

- Technical vocabulary
- Airport visit - interview staff and travellers
- Make your own passports
- Give information and directions to tourists
- Choose a holiday - using travel brochures
- Create a travel brochure
- Read timetables
- Research the history of flight/famous aviators
- Produce a book about a famous aviator or prepare an oral presentation using library research

GEOGRAPHY

- Maps/map reading
- Airport locations - local, national, international
- Air routes - distance/ time
- Air mail
- Air freight

PE

- Travelling through air and space

ART

- Models: seeds, planes, gyroplanes
- Kite patterns/pictures
- Collage of a windy day
- Frieze of an airport scene

▶ **RESOURCES**

art straws
balloon pump
balloons
card
centimetre squared paper
collection of fruits and seeds, including dandelion
  seeds, conkers, ash keys, horse chestnuts, sycamore
  seeds, field maple, etc.
hand lenses
hole puncher
newspaper
paper clips
Plasticine

polythene
polythene bags
Sellotape
string
sugar paper
tissue paper
Warmaline (thin polystyrene wallpaper lining)
washers
washing-up liquid bottles
wool

* tape recorder

Gyrating gyroplanes

Cut

Cut   Cut

Fold

Fold   Fold

Paper clip

Make a gyroplane.
Try it out.

Use your gyroplane to help
answer <u>one</u> of these questions.

What is the best number of paper
clips to put on the gyroplane?

Try making a gyroplane
from other materials.
Which material is best?

WHEN YOU HAVE FINISHED

Make up some questions about your gyroplane, such as:
'Does the shape of the wings affect how it falls?'
Make a list of your questions.
Find the answers to your questions.

1 Gyrating gyroplanes

Gyroplanes are great fun and allow the children to embark upon a wide variety of investigations. They can be made from a range of materials such as Warmaline, newspaper, card and tissue paper. This activity provides an excellent opportunity to assess children's ability to identify and handle relevant variables.

▶ Focus

In all investigations the children must be clear in their own minds, before they start, about what they are trying to find out. In the first investigation, the children are trying to find out whether the **material** of the gyroplane affects the **time taken** for it to fall to the ground. They will then have to consider two main questions:
- What do we need to change (the **independent variable**)?
- What do we need to measure to find out the effect of the change (the **dependent variable**)?

These are called the **key variables** in the investigation. (The children do not need to use these terms which are for teacher reference.)

They will have to measure the **time taken** for several gyroplanes (each made with a **different material**) to fall from the same height. Only by doing this will they be able to find the connection they require.

In the second investigation, the dependent variable is again the time taken, but this time the independent variable is the number of paper clips.

Ask the children to spend some time discussing what they plan to do. Encourage them to discuss what they are trying to find out, and what results they need to collect, before starting their investigations.

▶ FOLLOW-UP

The children could be encouraged to ask further questions and to find ways of answering them, for example:
- Does it work with only one wing?
- What happens if you double, triple, etc. the size of the wings?
- What happens if you halve or quarter the size of the wings?
- What happens if you launch it upside down?
- How could you make the gyroplane spin faster or slower?

▶ COMMUNICATION

* Produce a table of results.

Type of material	Time	Type of flight
Paper	2.47 seconds	Steady

* Present the data from the table as a bar chart.
* Make a tape-recording to describe how the investigation was carried out.
* As a group, decide how to display the different gyroplanes and the information gained from the investigations in an interesting way for a specific audience.

▶ CURRICULUM LINKS

MATHEMATICS
Recognise and understand simple fractions, e.g. be able to produce a gyroplane half or quarter the size of the original.

ENGLISH
Present data in tabular form for others to read.

Bouncing conkers

DID YOU KNOW THAT ...

Conkers are seeds from the horse chestnut tree.
On the tree the conkers are protected by
a thick spiky case.
The case is rubbery so that when it falls from
the tree it bounces away. Then it splits open
to let the conker fall out and grow in a
space of its own.

Make a collection of conkers.
Find out which conker travels the furthest.

Use a table to record your results.

2 Bouncing conkers

▶ USEFUL STARTING POINT

This investigation should be set in the context of research about trees in general, e.g. leaves, silhouettes, seasonal changes, bark, etc.

Discuss the mechanisms of seed dispersal with the children. Mention the fact that there are different methods of dispersal:
- wind dispersal
- water dispersal
- explosive dispersal
- animal assisted dispersal.

All of these methods are designed to send seeds away from the parent plant and improve the chances of germination and survival.

Horse chestnut fruits are made up of the seed itself (the conker) surrounded by a fleshy outer casing which protects it. The casing is rubbery and when the fruit drops to the ground it bounces and rolls like a ball before splitting open and releasing the inner seed. The conker itself can also bounce and roll. This is in contrast to those seeds which rely entirely on the wind to help them disperse.

Ask the children what might affect the dispersal of this seed, e.g. wind, surface water after a heavy rain shower, the nature and slope of the ground below, other plants in the vicinity, the presence of a stream, etc.

▶ Focus

During investigations the children have to make sure that their tests are 'fair'. In this case they must make sure that each conker is given an equal chance. It would be 'unfair', for example, if different conkers were dropped from different heights, or if they were thrown to the ground with different forces, or if they were dropped onto different surfaces. These things must be kept the same - they are called the **control variables**.

In this investigation the control variables include:
- the height from which the conkers are dropped
- the surface onto which they are dropped.

The children should be encouraged to discuss how they will make their tests 'fair' before starting any investigation.

▶ FOLLOW-UP

Allow the children to plant a horse chestnut seed to investigate the conditions under which it germinates. At a later date they may be able to plant their young tree in the school grounds and watch it grow, if this is appropriate.

If there is a suitable tree in the locality, the children could 'adopt' it and keep a record of how it changes through the year.

If time permits, they should be given the opportunity to drop conkers on different surfaces, e.g. grass, soft soil, hard soil, stones, and note any differences between how they bounce on each surface.

▶ COMMUNICATION

* Make a book about horse chestnut trees. A section on seed dispersal should include observations of the fruit, shape, texture, etc., as well as an account of the investigation. An explanation of why trees need to disperse their seeds, and how the horse chestnut tree accomplishes this, could be included.

▶ CURRICULUM LINKS

MATHEMATICS
Place information from the investigation into a database, then interrogate the database and draw conclusions from the data.

ENGLISH
Produce a booklet on horse chestnut trees and their seeds.

Make a super-parachute

Which is the best size for a parachute?

Which is the best shape for a parachute?

Use tables to record your results.

Use your answers to make a super-parachute.

3 Make a super-parachute

To construct a 'super-parachute' the children will need to investigate what features of a parachute affect the way it falls. Initially they are asked to investigate the following questions:
- Which is the best size for a parachute? (The teacher should insist on a quantitative reply rather than allowing the children to answer: a 'big' or 'little' parachute.)
- Which is the best shape for a parachute?
They can then use their results to make a super-parachute.

There are many ways in which this activity could be organised, for example:
(a) A group might decide to tackle each of the investigations in turn, analyse, interpret and draw conclusions from their results and then make the super-parachute.
(b) A group could sub-divide to investigate different parts of the activity sheet. Having completed their respective investigations, they could report back to each other and as a whole group make and test their super-parachute.
(c) The activity sheet could be used as a class starting point where groups either do the whole sheet or one part of it. Each group could record their results, analyse, interpret, draw conclusions and report them to the rest of the class. A class decision could then be made about which results should be used to create a super-parachute.

The children should be encouraged, however, to gather their results in a table which shows the following features:

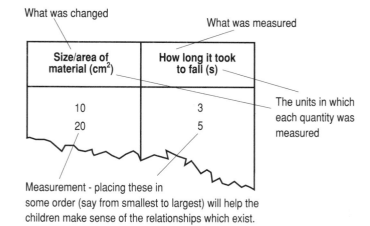

Measurement - placing these in some order (say from smallest to largest) will help the children make sense of the relationships which exist.

Children should always be encouraged to reflect on how knowledge and understanding can be put to use. In this particular activity, the children carry out initial investigations to broaden their understanding of the factors which influence the way a parachute falls. They must then use the extra knowledge which they have gained to produce the most effective parachute.

▶ Focus

Having carried out investigations to obtain the information they need, the children must then analyse and interpret their results. They may also need, in some cases, to prepare a report for other children in the class, or for some other audience, such as younger children.

Clear methods of recording, accompanied, where appropriate, by suitable forms of display, help the children to analyse and interpret the results which they collect. They also help them to recognise relationships and patterns where these exist.

There are many ways in which their results can be recorded and displayed, ranging from art and display poster work to formal tables with graphs or charts. They could include any models, with suitable annotations, where these are appropriate.

The form of recording which is used will depend on the nature of any follow-up work which is planned.

▶ COMMUNICATION

* Use tables when gathering data.
* Present tabular data in the form of bar charts.
* Produce a strip cartoon explaining how the investigation was carried out.
* Display results from separate investigations together to compare results.
* Suspend papier-mâché parachutes from the ceiling with investigation details hanging from them for other children to read.
* Use a computer program to store the data.

▶ CURRICULUM LINKS

MATHEMATICS
Choose and use appropriate units and instruments, e.g. read digital or analogue watches correctly.

ENGLISH
Give a presentation to others about how the parachute was made.
Write a report about the design of the parachute.

Magnificent paper planes

4

Design and make three different types of paper plane.

Carry out a test to find out which paper plane travels the furthest.

WHEN YOU HAVE FINISHED

Make a set of instructions to tell someone else how to make the paper plane which travels the furthest. Ask a friend to try out your instructions.

4 Magnificent paper planes

Ask the children to design and make three different paper planes using a limited range of resources. When they have made their planes, either jointly or individually, they should get together to decide which one is the best. The children might require some assistance in organising themselves to ensure that everyone in the group has a role in the making and testing of the planes.

After the group has tested the planes and chosen the best, ask the children to draw up a set of instructions to help someone else make the plane. The finished instructions should be a result of group collaboration, each child making some contribution.

►Focus

To make a paper plane begin to move through the air it must be given a 'push' - a force must be exerted on it. The aeroplane moves off in the same direction as the force which is making it move.

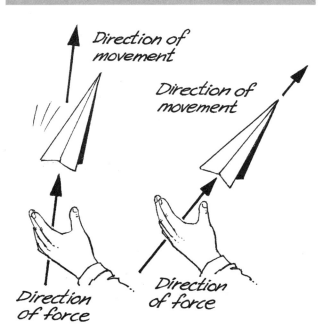

Direction of movement

Direction of movement

Direction of force

Direction of force

This basic principle, that forces make things begin to move, and that they move in the direction in which the force is acting, applies to everything which moves. For example, to throw a ball to someone it must be thrown with sufficient force to enable it to reach the other person (a larger force makes the ball travel further), and the force must also act in the direction in which you want the ball to move.

Alternatively, when ironing clothes, the iron is pushed to move it across the fabric. When it is pulled, it moves back across the clothes in the opposite direction because the direction of the force has changed.

Why does the plane fall to the ground? If a plane is dropped it will fall to the ground because it has weight (the force caused by gravity). This force (the weight) also acts on the plane when it is thrown into the air. After the plane leaves the thower's hand the only force (excluding air resistance) acting on it is its weight. If the thrower has thrown it upwards it rises slowly at first but soon begins to fall to the ground because of its weight.

► FOLLOW-UP

Discuss the results of their investigation with the children.
- Can they suggest why one model was better than the others?
- Was it the way the materials had been used or the shape?
- Was it the nature of the material itself?
- Could they suggest other materials which were not available but which might have worked better?

► COMMUNICATION

* Produce a table of results.
* Use the data from the table to prepare a bar chart.
* Prepare a set of instructions for someone else to use.

Plane	Distance travelled	Type of flight

► CURRICULUM LINKS

MATHEMATICS
Read scales using two decimal places to measure distance, e.g. 1.89 m.

ENGLISH
Find information from books about the historical development of aeroplane designs.
Write a test pilot's report.

Moving air

Air is all around us.
- **When the air is moving we call it a wind.**
- **When the air moves very gently we call it a breeze.**
- **Sometimes the force of the moving air is so big that we call it a gale.**

We can measure wind strength using an anemometer (say an-em-om-eter).

Card

Straw

Make your own anemometer.

WHEN YOU HAVE FINISHED

Use your anemometer to find out which part of the school grounds is the windiest.

5 Moving air

▶ USEFUL STARTING POINT

Discuss with the children how they can prove that air is all around them, that it moves and can exert a force. Let them brainstorm and list their ideas. Allow the children to try some of them. Their suggestions might include:

- running with an umbrella or piece of card

- blowing up a balloon

- making a blow football game or a game of 'flip-the-kipper'

- hanging a paper spiral from the ceiling over a radiator or near a door

- things they can see moving in the environment, e.g. shop signs, trees, street lighting, flags, washing, etc.

A discussion of these ideas could introduce the idea of being able to measure the force (or push) caused by moving air (the wind).   Ask the children to make their own 'wind strength' scale (say 1-5), using everyday descriptions such as:

1 calm - no movement

2 breezy - leaves rustle

3 fresh - branches move and litter is blown about

4 gale - whole trees sway and it is difficult to walk

5 storm - trees are blown down, buildings damaged.

The pupils are asked to make an anemometer using only a diagram as a guideline. Encourage them to discuss the instrument and to suggest how it will be made before they attempt to construct it. The pupils could calibrate the anemometer using their everyday descriptions of wind strength. This can be done by counting how many times one of the anemometer paddles goes round in 10 seconds for each everyday description of wind strength. For example:

Wind strength	Description	Number of turns in 10 seconds
1 2 3	Calm - no movement Breezy - leaves rustle	0 4

The final instruction suggests that the children use their anemometer to find the windiest parts of the school. Before the children begin, ask them to consider how they are going to record their observations. This could be in the form of a list or a map of the school onto which they can plot their findings.

▶ Focus

Why does the anemometer move when the wind hits it? Wind is moving air. Air is made up of very tiny particles of different gases, but the particles are far too small to see. If air particles strike an object in their path they push (exert a force) on it. Forces make things begin to move, so paper, leaves, boxes, even dustbins may begin to move. In really strong winds, such as gales or hurricanes, the force may be so big that it damages buildings or blows down trees.

As the moving air particles strike the vanes of the anemometer, they push against them. The vanes begin to move. The size of the force depends on the speed of the wind. Higher wind speeds produce bigger forces. So if the wind is moving quickly it exerts a larger force on the vanes of the anemometer, which makes it move around more quickly. By working out a scale for the anemometer (such as how many times it turns in 10 seconds), the wind speed at different times or at different places may be compared.

▶ FOLLOW-UP

Ask the children to collect magazine and newspaper pictures and articles showing the good and the bad effects of the wind, for example, the use of wind in certain sports and the destructive effects of a storm.

▶ COMMUNICATION

* Brainstorm a list of ways to prove that air moves.
* Produce strip cartoon instructions for making an anemometer. Include explanations of problems and possible solutions.
* Illustrate the five point adapted Beaufort scale using paintings or a collage.
* Draw a map of the school grounds and include readings from the anemometers to show the windiest and the most sheltered areas. Keep a table of readings taken around the school.

▶ CURRICULUM LINKS

MATHEMATICS
Select the materials and mathematics for a task. For example, make an anemometer and use it to test predictions about wind strength. Keep a record over a period of time.

ENGLISH
List evidence which shows that air is all around us. Present an account of the findings to others.

Incredible balloon rockets

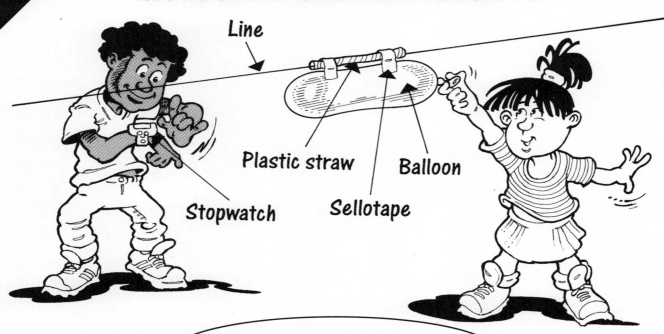

Line

Plastic straw

Balloon

Stopwatch

Sellotape

Make your own balloon rocket.
Use it to find out which is the best
material to use for the line.
You could try using:
• string   • wool   • fishing line
or anything else you can think of.

Draw a strip cartoon to tell other people:
• how you found out which line was best
• why you think one type of line is better than the others
• how a balloon rocket works.

MISSION IMPOSSIBLE!
Make a two-engine balloon rocket.

6 Incredible balloon rockets

▶ USEFUL STARTING POINT

The children need to develop the idea of air as a real substance. Ask them to blow up a balloon and describe what is inside it. Suggest that they feel the balloon - what can they feel? Let them release the end of the balloon - what happens? Can they feel something rushing out of the balloon? What is it? What happens to the balloon as the air rushes out? As the air rushes out it pushes the balloon forward. A balloon rocket can be used to demonstrate this, as shown on the pupil activity sheet.

▶ Focus

Forces make things begin to move. The force of the air rushing from the balloon pushes it forward. What makes the balloon slow down? As the balloon travels along, the sides of the straw rub against the wire or string which is supporting the balloon. Although these materials may feel fairly smooth, like most materials they look very rough when seen under a microscope.

As the two 'rough' surfaces rub against each other, they make a pushing force which acts in the opposite direction to the movement of the balloon. It is this 'pushing back' force (called the force of **friction**) which slows down the balloon. The rougher the surfaces, the bigger the pushing back force, so the balloon slows down faster, and does not travel as far. On very smooth surfaces the force of friction is much smaller, so the balloon does not slow down as quickly before stopping - it travels further.

Things slow down only when forces push against their movement. A bicycle slows down because the brakes push backwards against the movement of the wheels. The greater the slowing down force, the faster the bicycle slows down. This idea applies to all moving things.

The children can feel the frictional force of other materials and surfaces if they try to push their hands across them. Let them try to predict which surface is the roughest and which makes the biggest frictional force.

Ask them about the best surface for running certain toys along, and the most appropriate materials to use for the floors of the hall, classroom, sports hall, etc. Ask them why they can slide on an icy surface but not on the same surface when there is no ice.

▶ VARIABLES

It is important in any investigation that certain variables are controlled to make the tests 'fair'. In this investigation the relevant variables are:

Independent	Dependent	Control
Type of line	Distance moved by balloon or Time to travel a certain distance or Distance travelled in a certain time	Type (shape of balloon) Amount of air in balloon Method of fastening

▶ FOLLOW-UP

The children are asked to make a twin-engine balloon. This should be a problem-solving activity and the teacher should allow the children to try out their own ideas.

▶ COMMUNICATION

* Draw a strip cartoon to be used as instructions for someone else making a balloon rocket.
* Tape-record instructions or an explanation of the investigation - this could include sound effects.
* Word-process a description of the investigation, indicating the major problems faced, their causes and solutions.

▶ CURRICULUM LINKS

MATHEMATICS
Time an event using a digital stopwatch, reading it accurately to the nearest labelled division.

ENGLISH
Write a story about inventing a balloon rocket, describing feelings, emotions and the problems faced.
Label a diagram of the balloon rocket.

7 Make a Warmaline plane to travel 5 metres

Warmaline is a polystyrene wallpaper lining that is very light, thin, and easily cut and bent. It is available from DIY stores. Allow the children access to other materials such as Sellotape, art straws and Plasticine. The children should be allowed to design their plane before making it, although some children will work better if they can handle the materials directly and change their design as they go along.

▶ Focus

In any activity children should be encouraged, by effective questioning, to continually evaluate what they are doing in relation to the task which was set. In this activity the children will need to prepare a model plane, test it, note any deficiencies (particularly in relation to the task which was set), and consider how it could be improved. It should be a continuous process of evaluating the flight of their model in relation to the 5 metre brief. Children easily lose sight of the task which was originally set, allowing themselves to become sidetracked for a variety of reasons. Encourage them to reflect regularly on what they are trying to do by asking themselves the question 'How will this help me solve the problem?' At the end of all investigative work they should ask themselves 'Have I solved the problem? Could I have done it better if I had used another method? Could I have used other measuring instruments which were more appropriate? Have I got enough results to prove what I have found out?'

▶ FOLLOW-UP

The children could investigate and report on the following
- Which design is the most effective?
- Which is the best way to make the plane fly to the right or left?
- What happens if the wings are shaped differently?
- Which produces a better flight, a large or small force when launching the plane?

Plane	Distance flown	How it flew
Andrew's	3 m 65 cm	Flew straight then did a downward loop

▶ COMMUNICATION

* Produce a set of instructions, using words and pictures, to tell someone else how to make your plane.
* Create a flowchart of the stages in making and testing the plane.
* Test someone else's plane and produce a word-processed report on it. Include a table of results, pictures, etc.

▶ CURRICULUM LINKS

MATHEMATICS
Create a flowchart showing the stages in making and testing the plane.

ENGLISH
Comment on, discuss, and evaluate the construction of a friend's plane.

8 Find a way to send a 20 gram load 6 metres using air

► USEFUL STARTING POINT

Ask the children to make a list of the possible ways in which this problem could be tackled. The ideas put forward might be influenced by other activities in this unit which the children may have tried, e.g. 'Incredible balloon rockets'. Other ideas might include:
- balloon buggies
- sail buggies.

Suggest to the children that they keep notes as they work because at the end of their activity they will be asked to report to the rest of the class. When each group has finished making their report, other pupils should be encouraged to ask them questions.

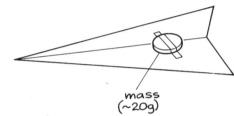

mass (~20g)

Paper plane

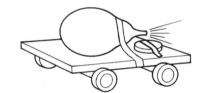

Balloon buggy

Sail- powered buggy

► Focus

There are many ways in which air can be used to carry a mass across the room. Some examples are shown in the diagrams.

Each of these suggestions uses the fact that **forces are needed to make something begin to move, and larger forces make things move further.**

When the children have designed their models, discuss the advantages and disadvantages of each one, paying particular attention to how the force was produced, and how the direction in which the mass moves depends on the direction of the force.

Ask the children to make simple suggestions in response to the following questions:
- How could they have made it move further?
- How could they work out how to make it travel 3 metres as accurately as possible?
If time permits, the children may then be allowed to test their suggestions.

► COMMUNICATION

* Make notes as a reminder of what happened during the activity.
* Work collaboratively to produce a report on the investigation for the rest of the class.
* Ask the 'audience', i.e. other pupils, to prepare their own questions to ask the children who gave the presentation.

► CURRICULUM LINKS

MATHEMATICS
Understand the relationship between two units of measure, e.g. centimetres and metres.

ENGLISH
Take part in a group discussion.
Prepare a group presentation for others in the class.

9 Make a collection of seeds. Find out which seed travels the furthest

▶ SAFETY

● Remind the children that some seeds are poisonous.

▶ USEFUL STARTING POINT

For this activity the children will need to be able to collect autumn seeds or have access to a collection. Discuss with the children why trees need to disperse their seeds. Ask the children to sort the different seeds into sets. Challenge them to explain the reasons for their classification and to say how they think the seeds in each set are dispersed.

The children should be encouraged to devise their own investigation to find out which seed travels the furthest. They should tabulate their results, then analyse and interpret them. Ask them to consider why some seeds travel further than others.

▶ Focus

The process of seeds moving away from the parent plant by one means or another is called dispersal. The seeds are dispersed in many ways, notably:
- by the wind
- by other animals
- by water
- by 'bursting' open, rather like an explosion, when the seeds are 'fired' away.

To help them stand a better chance of survival, they may have features such as 'wings' or 'parachutes' to help them be carried along by the wind, or they may have small 'hooks' which catch on the sides of passing animals.

Seedlings need water, good light, and nutrients from the soil if they are to grow strong. If the seeds fell near the parent plant there may not be:
- enough light (due to shading by the parent plant)
- enough water (most may be taken up by the parent plant, or the branches may shed water away from the area underneath)
- sufficient nutrients in the soil (most may be used up by the parent plant). Diseases can also spread more rapidly when plants are close together. However, there are disadvantages in moving away too, e.g. the seeds may land on the wrong type of soil, or in water, or on rocks. Or they may land in an area where there are already many plants. The competition for water, sunlight and nutrients may then prevent them germinating at all, or result in weak growth and early death.

▶ FOLLOW-UP

The pupils could research the life cycle of a tree. It is interesting to note that children do not always appreciate that all trees produce flowers at some time during the year. (The pollen from the flowers is one of the causes of hay fever.) The horse chestnut tree has very obvious flowers. Ask the children to find out what the flowers of other trees look like. Suggest that they present their information to the rest of the class. Ask them to think of an interesting way to describe the role of the flower in the reproduction of the tree.

▶ COMMUNICATION

* Produce a table of results.
* Present data from the table as a bar chart.
* Create a booklet about the life cycle of a tree.

▶ CURRICULUM LINKS

MATHEMATICS
Understand the notion of scale. Produce a diagram to scale, showing the distance seeds travel from the parent tree.

ENGLISH
Use reference material to find out information about the life cycle of a tree.
Describe the life cycle of a tree in a story, tape recording or poem.

Toybox

4 Robots

Robots can be made using recyclable material or from construction kits such as LEGO. The most important point is that the robot should fulfil the brief, i.e. have flashing eyes and lights on the control panel.

Children do not need instructions to make a circuit with lights in it. They will find their own way to make a suitable circuit if they are provided with a variety of materials and the opportunity to explore. Make sure they have a supply of the following: aluminium foil, art straws, batteries, brass fasteners, bulb-holders, bulbs, dowelling, drawing pins, elastic bands, lolly sticks, paper clips, Sellotape, switches and wire. Such a collection will allow the children to find out which materials allow electricity to flow (**conductors**) and which do not (**insulators**).

▶ Focus

When a battery is connected into an electric circuit, the chemicals inside it react with one another to give - **electrical energy**. (Energy can exist in many different 'disguises', or forms.) The electrical energy is carried around the circuit by tiny particles which are far too small to see. The flow of energy-carrying particles is called the **electric current** (just like the flow of water particles in a river is called a current). As these particles pass through a bulb, some of their energy is changed into **heat energy** and **light energy**. An electric circuit is a means of getting electrical energy from the battery to the components, such as bulbs, buzzers and motors.

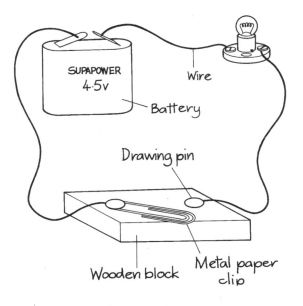

Bulbs need to be part of a complete circuit to work. A switch allows us to cut off the flow of electricity around a circuit. This cuts off the flow of electrical energy to the bulb. If there is no supply of energy, it cannot light. By moving the switch 'on and off' children will be able to make the bulbs flash.

In the diagram, the paper clip acts as a switch. As it is moved away from the drawing pin, it leaves a gap in the circuit. Since the gap is filled with air, and air is an insulator (electricity cannot flow through it), the bulb goes out. As the paper clip is moved back across to touch the drawing pin, electricity flows in the circuit once again and the bulb lights (because the metal of the drawing pin is a conductor - a material which allows electricity to flow through it). By moving the paper clip to and fro, the bulb can be switched on and off, giving the impression of flashing lights.

This kind of circuit, where all the parts are connected end-to-end in a line, is called a **series** circuit.

▶ FOLLOW-UP

When children have completed their robot, ask them to produce a simple drawing of their circuit. Some might be able to draw a proper circuit diagram using the following symbols.

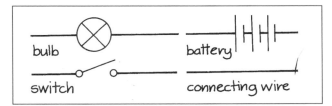

Ask the children to try using a switch in another position in the circuit. Does it make any difference?

▶ COMMUNICATION

* Draw a simple diagram of a switch system, or a more sophisticated circuit diagram of a circuit with a switch.
* Explain to another group how the robot's flashing eyes work.

▶ CURRICULUM LINKS

ENGLISH
Devise a drama about a robot which 'comes to life'. Give a verbal account of a robot entering the local village, perhaps in the form of an interview with an eyewitness.

Light up the house

Make a model house.

Give your house lights.

Find a way of switching each light off without switching all the lights off at the same time.

WHEN YOU HAVE FINISHED

Show your model to the rest of the class. Tell them how your circuit works.

5 Light up the house

Provide the children with a variety of materials and allow them to find out which are suitable for making a circuit with a light bulb in it. The bulb and battery should be similar, i.e. a 3.5 V bulb with a 3 V to 4.5 V battery - the same battery with a 1.25 V bulb quickly burns out the bulb. A selection of the following should be supplied: aluminium foil, art straws, batteries, brass fasteners, bulb-holders, bulbs, dowelling, drawing pins, elastic bands, lolly sticks, paper clips, Sellotape, switches and wire.

Challenge the children to:
- use suitable materials in their circuit
- ensure that wiring, etc., is hidden from view
- include more than one light in their circuit, for example wall lights, table lamp, standard lamp
- ensure that lights around the house are of a similar brightness.

▶ Focus

If bulbs are connected **in series**, electricity flows through one, then on to the next, then the next and so on. If a switch in the circuit cuts off the flow of electricity all the bulbs go out. (If lights in our houses were connected in this way, then switching a light on or off in one room would affect all the other lights in the house.)

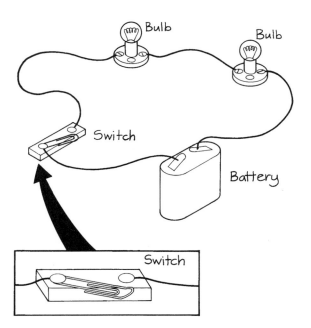

To switch bulbs on and off independently, they must be connected **in parallel**. In a parallel circuit all bulbs will light with the same brightness.

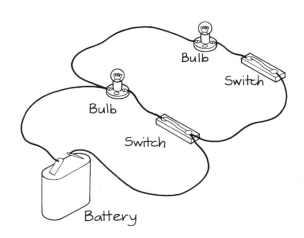

In this kind of circuit, the electric current splits up when it reaches the 'branch' in the circuit where the two bulbs are connected - some electricity goes through one branch, some through the other. By connecting separate switches in each of the 'branches', as shown in the diagram, individual bulbs can be switched on or off without affecting others.

▶ FOLLOW-UP

Take a length of lighting cable into the classroom. Ask why the cable has metal on the inside and plastic on the outside. Discuss this using the terms 'conductors' and 'insulators'.

▶ COMMUNICATION

* Discuss the danger of house and school mains electricity.
* Make a list of things to check if a light bulb does not work.
* Classify a set of materials into those that will allow a circuit to work (conductors) and those which will not (insulators). Present results using a table.

▶ CURRICULUM LINKS

ENGLISH
Write instructions for making a circuit, possibly using a word-processor.
Classify materials in the form of a table.

Shadow theatre

Design and make your own
shadow theatre and puppets.

• How do you make dark
shadows and lighter
shadows?

• Which material will make
the best screen for the
theatre?

THINK ABOUT

• Can you make
coloured shadows?

• How will you make your
shadows smaller or bigger?

WHEN YOU HAVE FINISHED

Write a play for your shadow theatre.
Perform your play for other children.
Tell them how shadows are made.
Tell them how shadows can be changed.

6 Shadow Theatre

▶ USEFUL STARTING POINT

Give the children a collection of materials, such as different types of paper, fabric, wood, polythene, etc., and ask them to sort them into three sets: transparent, translucent or opaque.

Ask the children to choose the most suitable material for a shadow puppet theatre screen from the set of translucent materials.

There are several ways of making a shadow theatre, one of which is shown below.

Ask the children to find out:
- how a shadow is made
- at what angle the torch should be held to make a shadow
- how far from the puppet the torch should be held
- how to make the shadow smaller or larger.

▶ Focus

Light is another form of energy. The children will most often 'see' light when it is produced by hot objects, such as the sun, or the filament in a light bulb. **Light energy** (unlike electrical energy) does not need anything to carry it from one place to another. It travels in the form of waves, and it can travel through space and through the air.

Some materials allow light to pass through them whilst others do not.

Transparent materials transmit a clear image. You can see through them clearly.

Translucent materials transmit light but it is scattered as it passes through them, so there is no clear image. You can only see vague shapes.

Opaque materials do not allow light to pass through them. Because the light cannot get through, you cannot see anything through these materials.

When an opaque object is placed in the path of a wide beam of light, the light passes around the outside of the object but is stopped where it strikes it. Light travels in straight lines so, if a screen is placed behind the object, the shape of the object (area of no

light) is clearly seen as a dark area, or shadow. The closer the screen is to the source, the smaller the shadow. The closer the light is to the source, the larger the shadow.
Some materials such as mirrors reflect light which strikes them. The light bounces off them and travels in a different direction.

Torch

▶ COMMUNICATION

* Sort a collection of materials and classify them as transparent, translucent and opaque.
* Display results in sets or in tables.
* Produce a shadow puppet play - word-process a script, make the puppets and perform the play. Explain to the audience how shadows are made and how they can be changed.

▶ CURRICULUM LINKS

MATHEMATICS
Make estimates based on familiar units, e.g. the size of a shadow.
Measure and draw angles to the nearest degree, e.g. at what angle should the torch be held?

ENGLISH
Write a play. Design a programme and tickets for the play.
Perform the play as part of a group presentation.

7 Which is the best washing-up liquid for blowing bubbles?

▶ USEFUL STARTING POINT

Ask the children to make a bubble-blowing set consisting of a bubble mixture and a bubble blower. Bubble blowers can be made from a variety of everyday objects, e.g. sieves, funnels, spoons with holes, or anything with a suitable hole in it. One of the easiest ways to make a blower is to create a simple loop in a piece of plastic-covered wire. Toy manufacturers produce a variety of basic and intricate bubble-blowing kits which the children may also enjoy using.

Ask the children to watch a bubble until it bursts. Can they tell you what happens just before it bursts? They should notice coloured patterns on the bubble's surface which look very like those which can be seen when a thin layer of oil floats on water. At this stage the bubble's walls have become very thin. Ask the children to suggest why a bubble pops - it is because water drains to the bottom of the bubble leaving the walls too thin to remain intact.

The children should then use their kit to answer the question 'Which washing-up liquid is best for making bubbles?' Before they begin their investigation, they will need to decide what they think 'best' means. The term 'best' might have a variety of meanings to different children, for example:

- the one that makes most bubbles

- the one that makes the longest lasting bubbles

- the one that makes the biggest bubbles.

▶ VARIABLES

The variables in this investigation are:

Independent	Dependent	Control
Type of liquid	Number of bubbles produced or Size of bubbles made or How long bubbles last	Amount of liquid Temperature of water Strength of blow Type of bubble blower

▶ Focus

The focus for this activity is on measuring the dependent variable effectively. Many children simply make qualitative judgements, for example 'That bubble solution is best because the bubbles last longest', without actually measuring how long the bubbles last. The children need to measure so that they can effectively compare one solution with another. In this case, because of the unpredictability of the bubble solution, they should be encouraged to make repeated measurements and to find an 'average' value for what they are measuring. Where children have difficulty calculating averages, they should be encouraged to select the middle number from a set of three. For example, in the set 6 seconds, 12 seconds, 10 seconds, the crude average would be 10 seconds.

▶ FOLLOW-UP

The children could investigate some of the following questions:
- Which shape of blower makes the best bubbles?
- Does the amount of water put into the washing-up liquid affect the number or type of bubbles made?
- Does the temperature of the water affect bubble making?

▶ COMMUNICATION

* Produce oral or written descriptions of their observations. The children should use technical terms such as transparent, rainbow, spectrum, flexible, soapy, detergent, temperature.
* Produce a star rating chart, giving different washing-up liquids one, two or three stars according to how good they are at producing bubbles.

▶ CURRICULUM LINKS

MATHEMATICS
Choose and use appropriate instruments - stopclocks, rulers, etc.
Handle data arising through experiments.

ENGLISH
Write a story, e.g. 'How I felt being trapped in a bubble'. Take part in a Rainbow Scavenger Hunt, collecting items for each colour of the spectrum, and record findings in an informative way.

8 Which toy car goes the furthest?

Many activities naturally engage one set of children more than others. In this case boys find the context helps them while girls frequently stand back and take a secondary role in mixed groups. The teacher should be aware of this possibility and be prepared to intervene to encourage girls to take a more active role.

▶ VARIABLES

The range of possible variables in this activity are:

Independent	Dependent	Control
Type of toy car	Distance travelled	Starting point Surface Method of starting

▶ Focus

The emphasis in this activity is firmly on developing the children's ability to carry out a complete investigation. The children usually find it easy to construct a fair test. The most difficult part of the activity is invariably having to handle the dependent variable, in this case how far the cars travel. Often children simply judge how far each car travels, and make statements such as 'The red car travelled further'. Conclusions such as this are fairly limited in what they say. They give no idea of how far the car travelled, nor of how much further than the others it travelled. To draw this sort of information from their investigation, the children should be encouraged to measure the distance travelled by each car, using appropriate measuring instruments. The teacher should demand precision in measurement from the children and ensure that they use (and include in their written accounts) the appropriate units.

▶ FOLLOW-UP

The children could be encouraged to raise their own questions about other factors which could affect how far the toy cars travel, for example:

- Which surface is best for cars to run on?
- Do heavy cars travel further than light cars?
- Which is the best way to slow a car down?
- Which is the best way to speed it up?
- What happens when a speeding car hits a stationary object?
- Does the angle of the slope affect the distance the car travels?

Different groups might tackle different questions and then report their experiences to the rest of the class, sharing their information and conclusions.

▶ COMMUNICATION

* List things to think about to give each car a fair chance (fair test).
* Produce a table of results.
* Give a talk to the rest of the class, or another group, describing your investigation.

▶ CURRICULUM LINKS

MATHEMATICS
Make estimates based on familiar units, e.g. estimating the distance which the car travelled before measuring. Measure and draw angles to the nearest degree, e.g. changing the steepness of the ramp.

ENGLISH
Give an eyewitness account of a road accident for the police, listing any details thought necessary.
Convey the results of an investigation in the form of a table.

9 Which ball is the best bouncer?

▶ USEFUL STARTING POINT

Make a collection of balls. Include golf balls, footballs, squash balls, tennis balls, plastic balls, sponge balls, etc. A rugby ball can be included for comparison. Ask the children to study each one carefully.
- What kind of material is it made from?
- Is it solid or hollow?
- Can you change its shape easily?
- Which one do you think will be the best bouncer? Can you suggest a reason why?

Ask the children for suggestions about how to measure the height of the bounce. Answers might include a chalk mark against a wall, a mark on paper, using an extended tape measure, etc.

▶ VARIABLES

The variables in the investigation are:

Independent	Dependent	Control
Type of ball	Number of bounces or Height of bounce or Type of bounce, i.e. straight, not at angle	Height from which it is dropped Method of release Type of surface

▶ Focus

The focus of this activity is on designing and carrying out an investigation. An important element of this is how the children record the information they collect. In this case the use of a table during the investigation would help the children to organise their numerical data. Once collected, the information could be presented as a bar chart. This should make it easier for the children to note any patterns or relationships in the data. For example, balls made from a certain substance may bounce higher than the others. Information in graphical form is often more meaningful than groups of numbers in a table.

▶ FOLLOW-UP

Having found out which is the best bouncer can the children suggest why that particular ball is the best. Do they think that it depends upon the size of the ball or the material the ball is made from? What else could affect how high it bounces? They could also investigate whether the surface makes any difference.

▶ COMMUNICATION

* Present a table of results as a bar chart. Many computer programs are designed to handle this type of information and can successfully represent tables as graphs.
* Produce a written explanation describing how the investigation was carried out and what conclusions the children came to.
* Produce a painting or a collage to show how the investigation was carried out. Include a word-processed description to accompany the work.
* Each child in a group could be given responsibility for one of these methods of communication. The whole group could then collaborate to organise a presentation of their work.

▶ CURRICULUM LINKS

MATHEMATICS
Use data from the investigation to produce a bar chart.

ENGLISH
Write a letter to the manufacturer enquiring how the ball was made.
Interview sports people about their sport.

The Lighthouse Keeper's Lunch

☐ **1 Foghorn**

☐ **9 Which material would make the best waterproof coat for the lighthouse keeper?**

☐ **2 Shine a light**

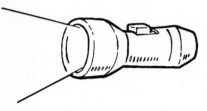

☐ **8 Make your own telescope using lenses**

☐ **3 Lunch to the lighthouse**

The Lighthouse Keeper's Lunch

☐ **7 The lighthouse steps are slippery in wet weather. Which type of shoe should the lighthouse keeper wear to be safe?**

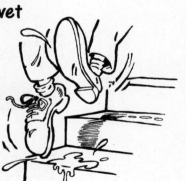

☐ **4 Life saver**

☐ **6 Weather watch**

☐ **5 Floating lifebuoys**

NAME:

Cross-curricular links

MATHEMATICS

- Collection of weather measurements
- Graphs to show weather measurements, e.g. bar graph for rainfall, line graph for temperature
- Timing using a digital stopwatch
- Coordinates on maps
- Measuring weight

TECHNOLOGY

- Design and make
  - a lighthouse
  - a round room
  - a lighting system
  - a model lifeboat
  - a lifebuoy
  - a telescope, and a platform to stand it on
- Create a system for exchanging parcels between a boat and the lighthouse
- Design a lunch menu for the lighthouse keeper
- Plan a healthy packed lunch for the lighthouse keeper at different times of the year, e.g. summer and winter

HISTORY

- Safety at sea through the ages
- History of lighthouses
- Famous sea rescues, e.g. Grace Darling

GEOGRAPHY

- Locate the nearest lighthouse on a map
- Use a large scale map of the British Isles and mark lighthouses around the coastline
- Lighthouses around the world, e.g. the most westerly lighthouse in Europe

The Lighthouse Keeper's Lunch

ENGLISH

- Send a message along a pulley system
- Retell the story of Grace Darling
- Write a poem about a lighthouse on a rocky shore
- Write a poem or story about the emotions of being on such an isolated post
- Create a diary of a lighthouse keeper, including daily chores, thoughts and emotions as well as rescues
- Describe conditions in bad weather
- Produce and tape-record a weather or shipping forecast for the radio
- Role play
  - a rescue at sea
  - a lighthouse keeper showing visitors around
  - receiving an SOS message

ART

- Build a papier-mâché model of a lighthouse
- Paint dramatic scenes of the sea
- Create silhouettes of a lighthouse against a night sky or a red sky
- Reproduce scenes from the story
- Create a picture book retelling the story

COMMUNITY LINKS

- Write to St Mary's House for information about lighthouses and coastal stations
- Visit a local lighthouse
- Interview someone who works at sea

▶ RESOURCES

aluminium foil	drum	wire
batteries	fishing line	wool
bells	pulley wheels	yoghurt pots
bulb-holders	range of elastic bands	
bulbs	range of hand lenses	* binoculars
buzzers	range of lenses, concave and convex	* The Lighthouse Keeper's Lunch
card	screwdrivers	by Ronda and David Armitage
cardboard tubes from kitchen rolls	springs	* camera
clear plastic bottles	string	* microscope
collection of fabrics	watering can	* tape recorder
cotton reels	weather instruments	* telescope
droppers	whistle	

5 Floating lifebuoys

▶ SAFETY

● Although this activity uses batteries, which are quite safe, remind children that they must never play with mains electricity, and that water and mains electricity are a dangerous combination.

▶ USEFUL STARTING POINT

Discuss the important features of a lifebuoy with the children. Ask them either to list these or mark them on a diagram of a lifebuoy. The children might suggest some of the following:
- it should float on the surface
- it should be visible from far away during both day and night
- it should have a light to warn ships of the danger
- it should be waterproof to protect the circuit inside
- it should be anchored to the sea bed so that it remains in the same position, i.e. where the danger lies.

There are a number of teaching points within this activity:
- electrical circuits - how to build a circuit within the buoy to make a light work?
- waterproof materials - the buoy will be in the water a long time, which materials will be the most suitable?
- floating and sinking - the ability to float will depend upon the materials used and the shape of the buoy.

The most important aspect is that at some point the teacher asks the children to explain the reasons for their choice of materials.

▶ Focus

The lifebuoy has weight - it pushes down on the water. If this were the only force involved the lifebuoy would begin to sink. Why does it float? There must be an equal force pushing upward. This force (called the upthrust) is made by the water which has been pushed aside by the part of the lifebuoy which is submerged. The more water which is pushed aside, the bigger the 'pushing up' force. The lifebuoy sinks until the 'pushing up' force balances out the pushing down force. When the two are balanced the lifebuoy floats. (When things are not moving there are balanced forces acting on them.)

Weight of lifebuoy (a downward force)

The 'pushing up' force of the water (the upthrust) balances the downward force of the weight. So the buoy floats.

▶ FOLLOW-UP

When the children have produced their lifebuoy, ask them to look critically at their model. Refer the children to their original list which suggested what the important features of a lifebuoy were. Does their model meet their original criteria? If not, how could it be improved?

▶ COMMUNICATION

* Create a working model in a plastic aquarium of the buoy anchored to the sea bed. Place diagrams, explanations, etc., of how the buoy works alongside the aquarium.
* Write a story describing how the buoy is serviced.
* Produce a diagram of the electrical circuit inside the buoy.
* Describe to other people how the buoy was made and explain:
 - how it is kept afloat
 - why it does not drift away from the danger point
 - how the light works and why the sea water does not affect the circuit.

▶ CURRICULUM LINKS

ENGLISH
Write a story about a storm at sea and how a lifebuoy helped to save the lives of a ship's passengers and crew.

Weather watch

DID YOU KNOW THAT ...

The lighthouse keeper gets weather reports every day. The reports tell him:

- wind direction
- wind strength
- types of clouds
- temperature
- rainfall
- visibility (how far you can see).

Design, make and use your own weather station.
Use your weather station to carry out a 'weather watch' for two weeks.

- What type of weather instruments should you have?

- Will you have to make any of your own instruments?

THINK ABOUT

- Where will be the best place for your weather station?

- How will you record the weather?

- Will you use symbols?

6 Weather watch

▶ USEFUL STARTING POINT

Discuss with the children how accurate weather forecasts are essential to a wide range of people such as:
- air-traffic controllers (who may have to redirect traffic due to fog)
- pilots (who can use a following wind to save fuel)
- motorists (who need to be warned of snow and blizzard conditions)
- farmers (who need to be warned of storms near harvest time)
- local authorities (who need to know when to grit roads in the winter)

The activity sheet asks the children to design and make their own weather station and to take regular readings over a period of two weeks. It suggests a range of questions which the children will need to consider before embarking on making their station. These include deciding what kind of observations they should make, for example:
- rainfall
- temperature (maximum and minimum)
- wind direction and strength
- visibility
- cloud type
- cloud cover.

Cloud cover can be estimated using a mirror grid. This is a mirror tile divided into grid sections using a felt-tip pen. The children use the mirror to view the sky and decide how much of it is covered by clouds. They can place the tile on the floor and shade in the corresponding squares on a paper grid.

For visibility, the children could make a simple scale based on how well they can see landmarks in the local environment.

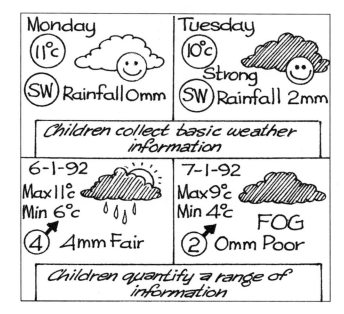

▶ Focus

The teacher may need to provide a more formal input on recording and communicating weather data. There are two main purposes for recording data:
(a) To record the type of weather experienced. The most effective way to show weather on a day-to-day basis is by using symbols. Children are familiar with weather symbols via the media. A video of a TV weather forecast is a useful way to introduce this type of recording. However, it is important that children begin to refine the symbols they use to represent an increasingly wider range of information. The example shown suggests progression in this area.

(b) To use data to note patterns and make connections. Children will need to develop a different set of recording skills if they are to make sense of weather data in terms of patterns. The use of graphs to show rainfall, temperature and wind direction and strength enables children to access and analyse weather data in terms of making connections between different sets of information, for example the relationship between rainfall, temperature and wind direction, or cloud type and rainfall.

▶ FOLLOW-UP

Video or tape-record a TV or radio weather forecast created by the children.

▶ COMMUNICATION

* Take weather measurements and display them in a table.
* Make a set of questions about the weather data for other children to answer.

▶ CURRICULUM LINKS

MATHEMATICS
Choose and use appropriate units and instruments in a variety of situations, interpreting number on a range of measuring instruments.

ENGLISH
Interview a visitor from a weather centre; formulate questions in response to information given by the visitor.

7 The lighthouse steps are slippery in wet weather. Which type of shoe should the lighthouse keeper wear to be safe?

▶ USEFUL STARTING POINT

Discuss some of the problems of working in and around the lighthouse with the children. One obvious difficulty is that during bad weather the steps to a lighthouse, and the rocks round about it, can be very dangerous. Encourage the children to think about what happens inside school on a rainy day when many of the floors become wet and slippery. Ask them which type of shoes they think are the safest to wear and to suggest reasons why (i.e. make 'I think ... because' statements). The reasons that children present will form their hypotheses some of which can then be tested.

▶ Focus

Our shoes grip on the ground because there is a force (called friction) between the soles and the ground. Friction pushes in the opposite direction to the movement of the sole over the ground. The force of friction is caused by the roughness of the surfaces.

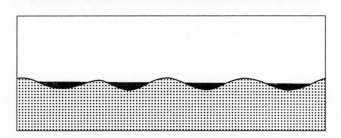

When the surface is wet, some of the roughness of the surface is filled by water - effectively 'smoothing it out'. The force of friction is smaller so we slip more easily.

The children can try pulling shoes or an object over dry and wet surfaces to see how easy or hard it is to move them. A newtonmeter can be introduced at this point if the instrument is unfamiliar to the children. Explain how this piece of equipment allows them to measure the pull which is needed (the force). It is important that children understand the need to quantify their observations. By giving the pulling force a number value, it is easier to make comparisons and come to useful conclusions.

▶ FOLLOW-UP

Discuss why cars and bicycles take longer to stop when the road conditions are wet or icy. The reason is the surface has less 'grip' so, even when the brakes are applied, it takes longer to stop. Ask the children to consider the implications for road safety.

▶ COMMUNICATION

* Produce a table of results.
* Produce a written account of the investigation, including what you were trying to find out, and what you found out when you had finished.
* Take rubbings of the soles of different shoes. Alongside each rubbing place an explanation of whether the shoe would be safe or unsafe to wear on a wet day.

▶ CURRICULUM LINKS

ENGLISH
Imagine that you are a shoe manufacturer and, in your best joined-up writing, you write a letter to the lighthouse keeper, describing your investigation and the type of shoe that should be worn in bad weather.

8 Make your own telescope using lenses

This activity can only be carried out if the children have access to a set of lenses that produce the right effect.

▶ USEFUL STARTING POINT

Provide the children with a collection of lenses to illustrate how looking through them can change the object they are viewing. Include in the collection some of the following: binoculars, drops of water, a glass jar, a microscope, a range of concave and convex lenses, a range of magnifying glasses, spectacles, a telescope, water-filled plastic lemonade bottles.

Asking questions helps to focus the children's attention. Some of the following questions might be incorporated in the display:

- Which is the strongest lens?

- What happens if you shine a torch through a lens?

- What is the difference between convex and concave lenses? What happens when you look through them?

- Can you find a way to use drops of water to magnify letters or words?

- How can you make a lemonade bottle magnify words or objects?

- Does the amount of water in a plastic bottle affect how it magnifies objects?

- Does the size of the bottle, its height or its circumference affect how it magnifies things?

This activity asks the children to make their own working telescope. Some children might wish to produce a design on paper. Others, however, will find it easier to handle materials and build a telescope on the basis of trial and error. They should notice how the distance between lenses has an effect on what they observe. Encourage the children to record their observations in tabular form, for example:

Distance between lenses	What the object looks like

▶ Focus

Real telescopes are very complicated and often make use of several different lenses. If the wrong lenses are used, or if they are used in the wrong order, then the image may be small (not magnified, or only slightly) or may be upside down.

Light passes through lenses. Convex lenses (those which are fatter in the middle than at the outside) form images (pictures) of whatever they are pointed towards. The children will be able to see an image if they stand well away from a window, point the lens towards the window, and move a piece of white paper to and fro on the side of the lens away from the window as shown in the diagram below.

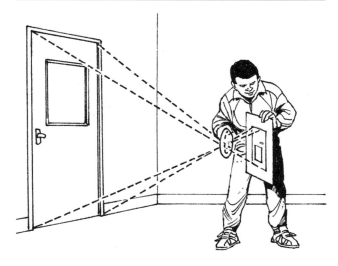

This image is invariably upside down. The second lens in a telescope turns this upside-down image around again, so that the final image is upright. The second lens also magnifies, making the image larger.

▶ COMMUNICATION

* Using different magnifiers, sketch what you can see through them.
* Make a booklet describing a range of things that can be used to magnify objects. Use pictures and words.
* Produce a set of instructions for making a telescope. Give the instructions to someone else to use. Ask them to decide how good the instructions were.

▶ CURRICULUM LINKS

ENGLISH
Describe to other children what the lighthouse keeper saw happening at sea through his telescope.
Write a set of instructions explaining how to make a telescope.

9 Which material would make the best waterproof coat for the lighthouse keeper?

Waterproof materials are meant to prevent water penetrating to the clothes underneath. Some may only be showerproof, i.e. they prevent light rain from penetrating but are ineffective in heavy rain. The children should be encouraged to design their own methods of testing different materials, and where appropriate quantify their observations by measuring how much water penetrates each material.

▶ VARIABLES

The variables in this investigation are:

Independent	Dependent	Control
Type of fabric	Amount of water fabric allows through	Size of fabric Amount of water Time Method of pouring water

▶ Focus

One of the main problems in this investigation is whether the children carry out the test effectively (or realistically). Most materials, for example, are likely to prove effective against a light shower. Sprinkling water (perhaps using a watering can) over the materials for 30 seconds, or even one minute, is unlikely to prove effective in any way. If, however, they simulate heavier rain, by using more water for a longer period of time, they will recognise the difference between a material which is showerproof and one which is waterproof. They should, however, be encouraged to quantify (make measurements of) the amount of water which soaks through each of the materials they test. Only by doing so will they be able to place them in order of effectiveness.

▶ FOLLOW-UP

Ask the children to look at the materials using a magnifying glass. Can they see any reasons why some materials are better than others?

▶ COMMUNICATION

* Create a chart using samples of the materials alongside data from the investigation.
* Produce a collage of a lighthouse keeper, using waterproof materials for his clothes.
* Produce an annotated diagram to show how the investigation was carried out and word-process information to go alongside it.

▶ CURRICULUM LINKS

ENGLISH
Write a poem about the lighthouse keeper.

The Baker

4 Super-loaf

► USEFUL STARTING POINT

Discuss the action of yeast in dough. Given the right conditions (food, water and warmth), yeast feeds on part of the flour and gives off gas bubbles which make the dough rise.

The activity sheet asks the children to find out if the amount by which the dough rises depends on the amount of yeast which is used. It is important that the teacher makes sure the children have understood the question before they begin their investigation. The teacher might ask:
- What does the question ask you to find out?
- What will you do?
- What will you measure?
- How will you make sure that your test is 'fair'?

Making large quantities of bread is wasteful. Encourage the children to make the mixture using a standard recipe and then divide it up into four or five batches, adding different amounts of yeast to each.

► Focus

Children find it difficult to appreciate that yeast is a living organism (it is actually a fungus), that it is alive and, like all living things, it needs food, warmth and water. Yeast is inactive when it is dry - nothing happens to it. When yeast is given water, warmth and food it begins to grow and multiply. The moisture is supplied by the liquid in the recipe. The food (initially) is provided by the small amounts of sugar in the flour. The warmth is provided by using warm water and by allowing the bread to stand in a warm place. It is the yeast which produces one of the changes which gives bread its 'light and airy' feel. As the yeast multiplies it changes and produces carbon dioxide gas . The gas is trapped in the dough, and forms 'gas pockets' which rise and make the dough swell. The dough must be allowed to stand for sufficient time to allow this to happen. (Like all living things the action of yeast depends on the temperature. If it is too hot, the yeast is killed and the bread will not rise. If it is too cold then it produces less carbon dioxide and the dough may not rise.

In unleavened bread there is no yeast and so the dough does not rise.

It is important that the children organise and record the data they collect in a way which will help them make sense of their results.

In this activity the children need to consider how much yeast to place in each sample. If the difference between each amount is too small, then there may be insufficient difference between the samples to enable them to draw any useful conclusions.

► VARIABLES

The variables here include:

Independent	Dependent	Control
Amount of yeast	Amount the dough rises	Quantities of all other ingredients Place where it is allowed to stand (or rise) Time for which it is allowed to rise Amount of dough in each sample How it is cooked

► COMMUNICATION

* Produce a table of results.
* Draw a strip cartoon to show how the investigation was carried out. The cartoon should show the results and conclusions.
* Produce a recipe page for a cookery book about how to make leavened bread. Include an explanation of why yeast is an important ingredient.

► CURRICULUM LINKS

MATHEMATICS
Select the materials and the mathematics to use for a task. Check results and consider whether they are sensible.

ENGLISH
Produce a recipe for others to follow, using complete sentences and appropriate punctuation.

Mouldy bread

What do you think makes bread go mouldy?

what makes bread go mouldy? IDEAS

In a group make a list of your ideas.

Choose one of the ideas from your list.

Design and carry out an investigation to find out if your idea was right.

5 Mouldy bread

▶ SAFETY

● The spores from mould can aggravate children who are asthmatic. Mould should only be grown under strict supervision. The method shown in the following diagram will eliminate any problems of this nature which may arise.

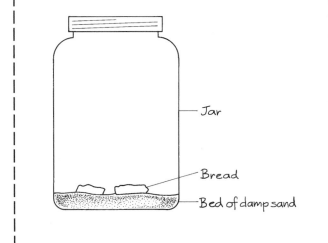

Jar

Bread

Bed of damp sand

▶ USEFUL STARTING POINT

Brainstorm suggestions about why bread goes mouldy. The children might suggest it depends on:

- the make of bread

- the type of flour which is used

- whether preservatives have been added

- whether the bread has been stored in the light or the dark

- whether the bread has been stored in a damp or dry place

- whether the bread has been stored in a warm or cool place

- whether germs or bacteria get on it.

The class could then split up, with each group choosing one idea from the list and investigating that particular idea. It is important that the children are given the opportunity to share information and conclusions with others at the end of their work. At the same time they should be encouraged to challenge the findings of other groups by asking pertinent questions about the data they have collected and their findings.

▶ Focus

Moulds are tiny fungi (living things). They are sometimes called **microbes** because they can only be seen, individually, using a microscope. They are always present in the air. Like other living things (such as animals, plants and ourselves) they need warmth, food and water. (Dehydrated foods have water removed. This prevents the growth of moulds.) They settle on food and multiply rapidly if the conditions are right. When they grow they can be seen as a fluffy coating on the food - we say the food has 'gone mouldy'.

Moulds grow most rapidly in moist conditions, and at temperatures between 20°C and 40°C. They grow on almost any type of food, although they grow more quickly on some foods than others. Moulds may multiply even in the low temperatures of refrigerators (cheese, for example, still goes mouldy even if stored in a refrigerator). Moulds also prefer foods which are slightly acid, such as jams and fruits.

The presence of moulds on food does not necessarily mean that it is unsafe to eat - merely that it is not fresh. Some special cheeses (such as blue cheeses) are made by encouraging moulds to grow in them. The moulds produce the characteristic taste of the cheese.

There are many different ways to preserve foods, such as vacuum sealing (removing air from the packets), freezing, adding chemicals, or removing water (as in dehydrated foods like dried milk). How do these methods affect the conditions (warmth, food and water) needed for living things to grow?

▶ COMMUNICATION

* Prepare an oral report for others in the class in which each person has a role. Describe the investigation and any conclusions which were drawn.
* Using the information gathered by the whole class, produce a leaflet for shoppers which describes the best way to keep bread fresh.
* Produce a strip cartoon explaining how and why mould grows on bread.

▶ CURRICULUM LINKS

ENGLISH
Create a 'mouldy' cartoon character that attacks bread. Write a story about how the character likes certain conditions.

Design a healthy sandwich

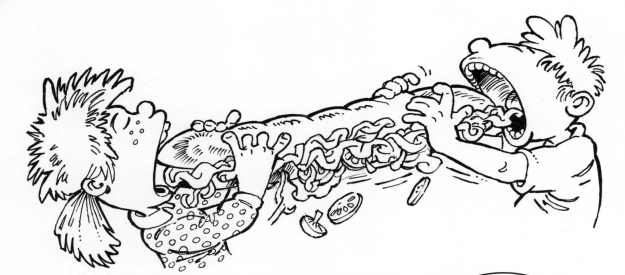

THINK ABOUT

• Which type of filling will be best?

• What type of bread will you use?

• Will you use butter or margarine?

• Does it look good enough to eat?

Draw a picture of your sandwich.
Label the different types of food in your sandwich.

WHEN YOU HAVE FINISHED

Show your picture to the rest of the class.
Explain to the class why you think your sandwich is healthy.
Ask your teacher if you can make your sandwich.
Does it taste as good as it looked in the picture?

6 Design a healthy sandwich

▶ USEFUL STARTING POINT

Make a collection of labels from different types of food which could be used in sandwich fillings, for example chicken, ham, cottage cheese, corned beef, etc. Include other foods such as hot-dogs and hamburgers.

This activity invites children to design a nutritious sandwich. It is important that children realise that although bread has its own nutritional value the filling can also enhance the nutritional value of a sandwich. The teacher could refer the children to the food labels and other literature, encouraging them to research the differences between different types of bread and fillings.

Discuss different aspects of sandwich 'design' that they must consider, for example:
- the sandwich must be popular with children
- the filling should have a high nutritional value
- some fillings will be more suitable for certain types of bread
- the sandwich should be firm and should not fall apart
- the sandwich should look appetising
- should butter or margarine be used?

Consider encouraging pupils to carry out consumer surveys to find out the type of sandwiches other children prefer. When they have designed their own sandwiches, they could carry out a further survey to find out how many children would eat it if it was offered in the dining-hall or snack bar.

▶ Focus

All food contains chemicals which we call **nutrients**. They are used by the body to help keep us healthy. The common names of the nutrients we need are:
- proteins
- carbohydrates
- fats
- vitamins
- mineral elements.

Different people need differing amounts of each essential nutrient. How much each individual needs depends on such things as age, sex, and how active the person is.
Many common diseases are caused by poor diets which do not contain the nutrients which we need. This is called **malnutrition**, and may be a result of **undernutrition** or **overnutrition**.

All 7 to 8-year-olds should eat (daily) food which provides:
- 9 kilojoules of energy (energy content is often shown on food labels)
- 53 grams of protein;
and the following minerals and vitamins:
- calcium
- iron
- vitamins A, C and D and riboflavin, niacin and thiamin.

Many of these nutrients are present in bread (some have to be included by law).

By looking at the labels from cereal packets and other foods commonly eaten, the children may be able to check whether they are getting the correct type of diet - one which provides these essential nutrients.

▶ FOLLOW-UP

The children could interview someone from the school meals department to find out what steps they take to make school meals nutritious and part of a 'healthy diet'.

▶ COMMUNICATION

* Produce a class sandwich recipe book. Encourage children to use a variety of methods of recording, e.g. diagrams, writing, poems, photographs, strip cartoons, and to include hygiene instructions.
* Create a poster advertising 'New Scrumptious Sandwiches' and describing their nutritional value.
* Produce a poster for the dining-hall promoting 'Healthy Eating'.

▶ CURRICULUM LINKS

ENGLISH
Produce posters and recipe books using correct spelling, punctuation, etc.

7 Use LEGO to build a working windmill.

LEGO Technic is one of the obvious choices for making this type of model. A battery-powered motor could be used to drive the mechanism. It is important that the children are challenged to fulfil the brief which asks for a working model. Equally important is that, when the model has been constructed, the children are given opportunities to discuss the scientific ideas which are involved.

▶ Focus

Natural resources such as wind and water have been used for thousands of years (and are still used in many countries) to grind the seeds which make flour. The advantages of these natural resources are that they do not cause pollution in any form and unlike other energy sources they will not run out.

Gears and other types of mechanism are used to pass on the forces (and energy) from the sails of a windmill, or the paddle of a waterwheel, to the parts which grind the seeds to make flour.
When the children have completed their task, focus attention on the way the different parts of the mechanism pass on the forces, and particularly on any changes of **direction** which take place.

Energy is produced whenever forces make things move. (Energy is needed to make things work.) In a windmill the energy from the wind (moving air) makes the sails move. The energy is then passed on by different parts of the mechanism, eventually reaching the stones which grind the corn. (Some of the energy is lost as heat because of friction as the different parts of the mechanism move over one another - the more moving parts there are, the more energy is lost.)

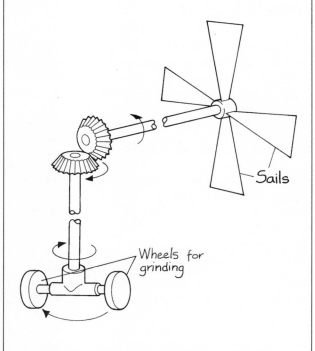

This schematic diagram shows the direction of forces which turn the wheels of a windmill model

▶ COMMUNICATION

* Produce a diagram for other children to use showing how your model was made.
* Produce a diagram to show the direction of the forces which turn the wheels in your model.

▶ CURRICULUM LINKS

ENGLISH
Draw and annotate a diagram of the model windmill.

8 Grow your own wheat. Keep a diary of the changes

The children are rarely given the opportunity to grow a plant, observe its complete reproductive cycle and help to begin the cycle again. This is an important concept - the cyclical nature of growth. In the environment, it is determined largely by the changes in the seasons. If the children are to be able to grow wheat and collect the seeds, it must be sown early enough in the school academic year to allow it to mature to produce grain. It will also need a sunny place.

Ensure that the seeds are planted in a large pot (25 cm) and that the children tend the plants regularly, making sure they have sufficient water and fertiliser (fertiliser, given at regular intervals, will help provide the growing plants with the extra nutrients they need). Ask the children to keep a shared class diary of both quantitative and qualitative observations of growth.

Alongside the main crop, children might set up investigations to find out whether any of the following affect growth:
- temperature
- light
- water.

▶ Focus

Most plants, including those we grow for food, have an annual cycle which depends on the seasons.
- In spring the seeds are planted as the ground warms up and the days become longer. The seeds need warm, moist conditions to germinate, or begin to grow. As they germinate the seeds use their own store of food (which is held inside the seed coat) to grow.
- In summer new growth flourishes and flowers are produced. Sunlight changes chemicals inside the plant into the food which it needs to grow. The eggs are pollinated by insects or the wind and the new seeds begin to form.
- In autumn the crop is harvested (the seeds are gathered). Some of the seeds are used for food. Others are stored for planting the following year.
- In winter the old growth dies. If it is allowed to rot in the ground it provides humus and some of the nutrients which help make the soil fertile (suitable for strong growth).

▶ FOLLOW-UP

Ask the children to research information about other types of crops (e.g. oats, chick peas, barley, rice, wheat or corn), particularly those which are grown for food in other countries. Pupils should find out if the growing cycle and the seasons are similar to Britain.

▶ COMMUNICATION

* Keep a diary to note changes in growth over a period of time.
* Give a talk to the rest of the class about another crop from a different country, describing the stages of growth in that plant.

▶ CURRICULUM LINKS

ENGLISH
Give a talk to the rest of the class about different types of crops around the world.

9 Making bread. What happens if you use different types of flour? Find out which flour is best

▶ USEFUL STARTING POINT

Make a collection of different types of flour. Include as many of the following as possible:
- plain flour
- self-raising flour
- maize flour
- ata flour (wholemeal flour)
- barley flour
- brown flour
- white flour
- strong white flour.

Challenge the children to list as many similarities and differences as they can between the different types of flour. Hand lenses or a microscope will help enhance their observations.

They should then be asked to make bread using the different types of flour which are available. To reduce waste the children could calculate how much flour would be required for mini-loaves and also how much of the other ingredients are required, reducing each of the ingredients by the same proportion. This would allow children to make smaller loaves but still be able to contrast and compare the final products.

The children might decide to compare two different types, for example brown and white flour or white flour and wholemeal flour. Their conclusions could be based on quantitative data such as the size of the loaves, or also include qualitative observations such as the appearance and taste of the bread.

▶ Focus

We should all have a healthy diet. Healthy diets can help reduce some of the health risks in later life, and also ensure that our body is able to function properly on a day-to-day basis. Dietary fibre is an essential part of any healthy diet. Bread can provide some of the fibre which our bodies need to function effectively.

White bread	Wholemeal bread	Brown bread
1g per slice	3.5g per slice	2g per slice

Different types of flour contain different amounts of fibre. The table shows the amount of fibre in bread which is made using different types of flour.

Other foods which contain a high proportion of dietary fibre are:
- some cereals, such as bran and muesli
- baked potatoes
- baked beans
- dried fruit and pasta
- fresh fruit
- peanuts, rice and most other types of nuts and seeds.

The average person should (it is recommended) eat at least 30 grams of dietary fibre each day. How do the children fare? Eating plenty of bread, particularly wholemeal or brown bread, can go a long way towards providing the fibre they need.

▶ FOLLOW-UP

Involve the children in an information search. Using leaflets and books, they could find out if there are nutritional differences between different types of flour. Is white flour better than wholemeal flour. If so, why? What is their intake of fibre each day? Is it sufficient? If not, what can be done to improve matters? Ask the children to carry out a survey of eating habits within the class and the school.

▶ COMMUNICATION

* Describe the differences between types of flour when they are viewed under a microscope.
* Explain to other children what bread is like when it is made using different types of flour.
* Set up a mystery tasting session. Can friends guess which type of flour was used? They must explain their reasons.

▶ CURRICULUM LINKS

MATHEMATICS
Mentally calculate the changes needed to a recipe to make smaller quantities.

ENGLISH
Listen to the views of other children about their preferences about the type of flour used in bread or about the information they have found out about bread.

Animals

☐ **1** How big is a minibeast?

☐ **9** Where do you think woodlice like to live? Do you think they like to live in sunny, shady, damp or dry places? Carry out a test to find out if your ideas were right

☐ **2** What lives in the garden?

☐ **8** Design a mini-garden that will encourage animals to live there

Animals

☐ **3** Bird watch

☐ **4** 20 questions

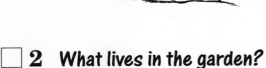

☐ **7** Explain the life cycle of an animal in your garden or school grounds in an interesting way to other children

☐ **5** Habitats

☐ **6** Make a food web

Blackbird   Thrush

Worm   Snail

NAME:

Cross-curricular links

Animals

ENVIRONMENTAL EDUCATION

- Habitats in the locality
- Human influences on the environment from creating wild areas to destroying a hedgerow
- Controlling garden 'pests' - discuss alternatives

MATHEMATICS

- Use and create keys
- Measuring dimensions of invertebrates
- Tables of results
- Producing graphs, e.g. distribution of invertebrates
- Tally charts
- Comparisons using the *Guinness Book of Records*

TECHNOLOGY

- Re-create a habitat in the classroom to house, for example, woodlice
- Design and produce a 3-D model of an ecosystem, e.g. under a stone, in a hedgerow
- Design and make a weighing instrument
- Design a garden to encourage different types of animals
- Design, make and test a bird feeder

ART

- Drawing using different media, e.g. charcoal
- Appliqué or cross-stitch pictures of invertebrates
- Clay models of invertebrates
- Using patterns, e.g. snail shell, to create abstract pictures

DRAMA/MOVEMENT

- Mime/role play - different animals - fear of invertebrates - persuading someone not to destroy an animal or habitat

GEOGRAPHY

- Mapping skills - plotting location/distribution of animals around the school grounds
- Invertebrates in different countries
- Crop infestation and destruction, e.g. locusts in different countries

RE

- Attitudes towards animals
- Animals in different religions
- Caring for living things and the environment
- Personal and collective responsibilities

HEALTH EDUCATION

- Head lice
- Animals (e.g. flies, dogs) as carriers of disease (e.g. rabies, toxicara)
- Infestation, e.g. cock roaches, mice
- Handling of pets

MUSIC

- Mimicking sounds
- Designing and making instruments to mimic sounds
- Teach rhythm (e.g. crochet, quaver, minim) through the movement of animals, e.g. crochet - walking (wood louse), quaver - running (spider), minim - slow steps (snail)
- Imagine that an invertebrate is crawling over an instrument - what would the music be like?

ENGLISH

- Reading poetry about animals
- Writing poetry based on close observation
- Annotate sketches using descriptive language
- Create an animal life cycle video
- Produce a nature radio broadcast
- Develop reference skills to research additional information about animals
- Formulate a range of questions and then decide the method to be used to find answers

RESOURCES

bird food	plastic aquaria	thermometers	* binoculars
clay	plastic lemonade bottles	wool	* camera
disposable plastic gloves	plastic sweet jars	world map	* reference material, e.g.
hand lenses	Plasticine	yoghurt pots	books, leaflets, charts, videos
paintbrushes	string		* tape recorder

5 Habitats

This activity asks the children to choose two habitats and compare them and the animals living there. Through direct comparisons they can note similarities and differences more easily. It might also enable them to realise how some animals and plants have specifically adapted to one locality and why they would be unable to survive elsewhere. The choice of habitats does not necessarily require children to work away from the school surroundings. For example, they could compare a wall habitat with a tree habitat. Other suggestions for habitats are:

hedgerows   soil   ponds
under stones   grass   fencing

The children should explore each environment and note the characteristics which make them different. This should include taking appropriate measurements. Examples of characteristics include:

light   temperature   moisture   wind
soil   vegetation   animals   plants

daily changes, e.g. amount of light
human influence, e.g. cultivated, human movement nearby.

Habitats can be small or large. Under a stone is a habitat - it supports a community. The stone might be part of a larger habitat such as a hedgerow which will undoubtedly support a far greater variety of plant and animal life. The children are asked to suggest why the animals like their environment. This will require careful observation by the children.

▶ Focus

A habitat is a place where plants and animals live. One habitat may be quite different to another. Some habitats are in dry and sunny places. Others may be damp and shaded. Some may have lots of vegetation. Others may have little vegetation and may be composed of a little soil, sand and stones. The animals which choose to live in a particular habitat do so because it provides the right conditions for their particular needs. They are adapted to live in certain conditions and to eat specific types of food. The changing seasons, changes in the pattern of night and day, and the complicated webs of food chains all have an effect on the lifestyle of the animals in any habitat.

This activity provides an opportunity to explore with children the idea that certain animals prefer particular types of habitats and that the differences in location around a garden or school ground are often reflected in the living things (including the plants) found there. Discuss how the chosen habitat of each of the animals found depends on:
(a) the physical characteristics of the animal, and/or
(b) what it eats.

By choosing quite different habitats we should find different species of animals. When studying the habitats the children should be encouraged to look for similarities and differences between the plants and animals which they have found. In what way are they suited to the conditions in which they live? They should be looking for connections between the features of the plants or animals, and the characteristics of the habitat. They should think about and interpret what they see by considering questions which reflect relationships in their observations, for example:
- How many different types of animals can they find in each habitat? What do they eat and how does the habitat meet those needs?
- What would happen if the habitat was changed in some way, such as if the vegetation was removed, or if someone killed off some of the animals by carelessly dumping chemicals?
- Do plants which live in dry places have smaller leaves than those which live in damp places (to reduce the amount of water lost)?
- Do snails live only near walls or other types of stone (so they can get the calcium they need to maintain their shells)?
- Is there a connection between the type of animal found in a specific habitat and the other types of life found there, e.g. do snails prefer areas where there is plenty of vegetation?
- Do plants in dry areas have wider root systems than those which live in damp areas (so that they can draw as much water as possible from the little they receive)?

▶ COMMUNICATION

* Make sketches and notes of the different habitats.
* Take photographs of the different habitats.
* Using sketches, notes and photographs, create a collage of the habitats.
* Give information about the way in which an animal has adapted to its habitat. This could be in the form of a drawing, word-processed text or a tape recording.

▶ CURRICULUM LINKS

MATHEMATICS
Choose and use appropriate measuring instruments, e.g. thermometers.

ENGLISH
Research information from books about the different animals in a habitat.
Write a story for a younger audience about an animal, where it lives and what happens to it, e.g. 'A day in the life of a ...'.

Make a food web

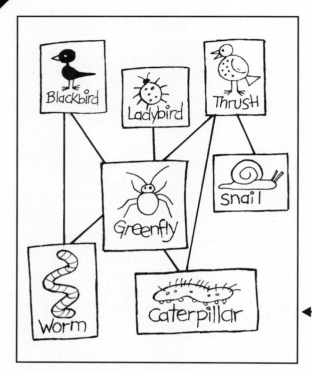

Make a list of all the
animals you can see
in the school grounds.

Draw pictures of
all the animals
in your list.

Make a display using your pictures.
It might look like this.

Which animal in your display
is a predator? (A predator kills
and eats other animals.)

Which animal in your display
is the prey? (Prey are killed
and eaten by other animals.)

Join the predators to their prey by
drawing lines or using string.
You might have quite a tangle.
You have made a food web.

What would happen to the food web
if one of the animals died off completely
and there were no more of them
in the school grounds?

6 Make a food web

Children need to understand the very complex relationships that exist in a garden or in the school grounds. The activity sheet asks the children to make a list of the animals observed in the school grounds. They should then produce sketches, or models, of these animals for display. Where an animal eats or is eaten by another a link can be made using thread, string or wool, etc. A symbol could be used to indicate the predators in the food web or the different types of consumers, such as:
- carnivore   (feeds on other animals)
- herbivore   (feeds on plants)
- omnivore   (feeds on plants and animals)
- detritivore (feeds on decaying plants).

An example of a food web is shown on the activity sheet. The children could plot different food webs which exist in a variety of habitats, for example a wall, hedgerow, tree, stream or grass.

▶ Focus

In any habitat there is a system of food supply which is carefully balanced to meet the needs of the animals that live there. This system is called a **food web**.

Animals need food to provide them with the energy they need to survive. Some eat vegetable matter. Others eat other animals which may themselves have eaten plants. Perhaps the most important difference between plants and animals is in the way they get the energy they need.

Plants get their energy from the sun. Animals get their energy either by eating plants, or by eating other animals which may have eaten plants. For example, foxes eat rabbits and rabbits eat grass and other plants. This is a simple **food chain:**

grass ────────▶ rabbit ────────▶ fox

But real life is not as simple as this. The grass, for example, feeds other animals. Other animals, such as golden eagles, may also eat rabbits. Our single food chain then combines with other food chains to create a **food web**.

A food web may look like this:

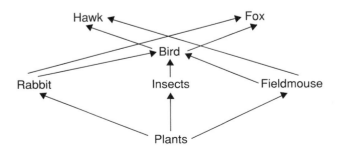

If one type of food became scarce, then it would have an effect on other parts of the food web. If, for example, the rabbit population suddenly decreased, foxes would have to eat more of the other small animals, such as mice. There would be fewer for the hawk to feed on, so the hawk would possibly eat more small birds. If there were fewer birds, then the insect population could increase dramatically, damaging crops and other plants.

The children should begin to realise that food webs are complicated and that they change as circumstances in the environment change. By looking at their food web they should recognise that some of the animals and plants appear only at certain times during the year. This affects the life cycle of other living things.

A shrew, for example, feeds on worms. During the winter months worms burrow deep below the surface to protect themselves from the cold. As a result there are no worms for the shrew to feed on. Because it cannot get food, it must retain as much of its body energy as possible during these lean times. It hibernates in a warm dry place, conserving its energy.

For similar reasons, the young of many animals are born only when food supplies are plentiful. If they were born at times when food was difficult to obtain, then many would probably die.

Ask the children to think about what would happen if any one part of their food web was destroyed. Would any of the species disappear because their sole source of food no longer existed? If not, which other part of the food web would be in greater demand as animals compete for the reduced food supply?

▶ COMMUNICATION

* Produce models, paintings or drawings of predators. Place them on a display and show how each one fits into the food web using thread, wool or string.
* Build a model of a habitat indicating the different animals living there and their relationship in the food web.
* Make a list of predators and match their prey to them.
* Design and make a game of 'predator/prey snap', where players have to match the correct predator to the prey.

▶ CURRICULUM LINKS

ENGLISH
Write a poem about an animal catching its prey. The poem could be written from the point of view of either the predator or the prey.

7 Explain the life cycle of an animal in your garden or school grounds in an interesting way to other children

Throughout *Science in Action - 5 to 16* children are encouraged to use a variety of sources of information. Where they use such secondary sources it is important that they are challenged to present the information in another way. This helps to overcome the problem of children copying information without really understanding it. If they are asked to present the facts in a different manner for a specific audience, then they are more likely to develop a better understanding of them. For this reason the activity requires children to find an interesting way to explain the life cycle of an animal from their own garden or school grounds. This is also a method of extending a child's understanding of an animal he/she might have collected and housed in the classroom.

Children could present information in the form of books, life cycle wheels, video recordings, strip cartoons, collages, models, or they could make an oral presentation to a specific audience.

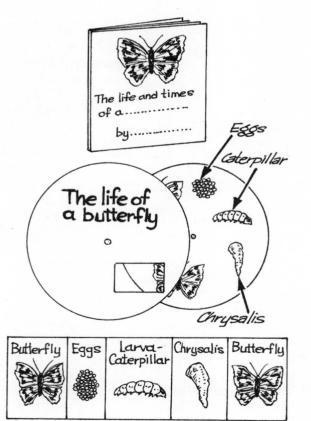

▶Focus

An important point about life cycles which the children frequently miss is that they are cycles and they repeat with each new generation. Discuss with the children the cyclical nature of reproduction. They should also begin to develop an understanding of the timing of animal life cycles (see previous activity). Most are timed to occur when conditions are right, in particular when food is available, to ensure that the young survive. The children should also realise that life cycles are dependent on habitat. Many animals can only survive and reproduce in very specific conditions. If the habitat is disturbed or destroyed then some species will not survive.

▶ FOLLOW-UP

Provide the children with a context which would lead to them discussing human influences on the environment. This could provide an opportunity for role play if the children are given a suitable context. For example, a farmer wants to remove a hedgerow to increase crop yields, or a new road is planned which will destroy land on which rare butterflies breed. The children should be able to provide arguments for and against this type of development, with particular reference to the way it could affect the life cycle of the animals that live there.

▶ COMMUNICATION

* Create a painting about the life cycle of an animal.
* Produce a collage to show the different stages of an animal's life cycle.
* Make a set of models of the life cycle of an animal found in the school grounds.
* Create a model habitat in which the different stages of a life cycle are shown.
* Produce a tape recording with a handbook explaining the life cycle.
* Role play a public meeting debating, for example, the construction of a new road through an area where a rare species of animal lives.

▶ CURRICULUM LINKS

ENGLISH
Write a story sequence of the life cycle of an animal. Place the written sequence alongside a set of pictures. Create and annotate a diagram of the life cycle of an animal.

8 Design a mini-garden that will encourage animals to live there

▶ USEFUL STARTING POINT

Ask the children to make a list of the different types of habitat which they might create in a small space in order to encourage animals to live there or to visit it. They could be given or asked to collect information about their particular area and encouraged to make suggestions based upon the conditions there, e.g. very shady or very sunny.

The children should keep their ideas simple. They could suggest, for example:
- making a bird table
- creating a rockery where there are stones for animals such as woodlice to live
- having a wood pile for woodlice and fungi
- growing flowering plants or shrubs, e.g. buddleia, to encourage insects such as butterflies.

Invite the children to plan out their mini-garden using drawings, sketches, diagrams or a model. They should include descriptions of the different parts, naming the plants to be grown and the type of animals the area might attract and why.

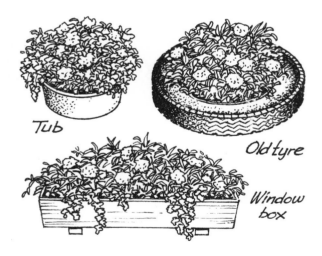

Tub

Old tyre

Window box

Ask the children to keep a diary of the development of their own area, logging the gradual change using notes, photographs, plans and sketches.

The time of year will play an important part in whether or not planting a garden is feasible.

▶ Focus

Before planning a mini-garden, particularly one which is designed to encourage specific animals and plants to live there, the children will need to consider:
- What type of animals do they wish to attract? This may affect the type of plants they grow.
- What conditions do they require, i.e. what are the characteristics of the natural habitat of these plants and animals (sunny, shady, damp)?
This planning needs to be carefully done to ensure any degree of success.

Useful information can be obtained from:
- book and library research
- a visit from a Conservation Officer
- a visitor from a local garden nursery
- literature from environmental groups and conservation societies.

▶ COMMUNICATION

* Produce a plan of the garden area for display.
* Word-process information about the different plants, areas, etc., and add it to a display which includes the original plan.
* Keep a diary of changes.
* Take photographs of each stage when creating the garden area. Produce an album with descriptions to accompany the photographs.
* Use tables to record the type of animals visiting the area.

▶ CURRICULUM LINKS

MATHEMATICS
Create a scale drawing of a mini-garden.

ENGLISH
Produce a plan of the garden area for display.
Keep a weekly diary of changes observed in the garden area.

9 Where do you think woodlice like to live? Do you think they like to live in sunny, shady, damp or dry places? Carry out a test to find out if your ideas were right

▶ SAFETY

● Children should not handle invertebrates directly, particularly those found in the soil, due to the increasing risk of toxicara and other soil-borne diseases. To promote safety it is advisable for children to wear disposable plastic gloves, to always scrub their hands and fingernails whenever they have been working with invertebrates, and to avoid touching their faces with their hands whilst working.

Before the children begin this activity they need to understand that all living things deserve care and attention. If woodlice are collected then a soft paintbrush could be used to brush them gently into a yoghurt carton. This is a considerate way to collect such specimens. As the children are collecting woodlice they should make a note of the habitats in which the animals were found using sketches and jottings.

Discuss with the children where the woodlice were found and encourage them to describe the conditions. Ask the children to plan an investigation to find out if woodlice do prefer the conditions they described.

▶ Focus

Many animals, such as worms and snails, cannot survive long in strong sunlight and high temperatures. During daylight hours they must remain in shaded places, or underground. Other small creatures are only found on the shaded underparts of leaves, where they gain some protection from the sun's rays. Other animals may feed during the evening or at night because they feed on other animals (their prey) which may be nocturnal themselves.

When the children intend keeping woodlice for any length of time within the classroom they should think about how to house them in conditions which are similar to their natural habitat. At this point refer the children to the results of their investigations and their original sketches and jottings of woodlice habitats. This helps them to reflect on the natural conditions under which woodlice live and how those conditions might be re-created in the classroom. Woodlice enjoy dark, damp conditions so their housing might resemble that shown in the diagram.

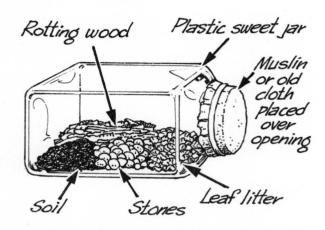

Rotting wood — Plastic sweet jar — Muslin or old cloth placed over opening — Soil — Stones — Leaf litter

* Woodlice habitats must be kept damp. Plant sprays are excellent for keeping the habitat moist.

▶ FOLLOW-UP

Encourage the pupils to carry out a literature search to find five fascinating facts about woodlice and to create a 'Did you know...?' display alongside the classroom habitat with information from their investigation. They might discover facts such as: woodlice are the only land-living member of the crustacean family and are distantly related to shrimps and lobsters.

▶ COMMUNICATION

* Produce a map of a garden or the school grounds. The map might include information about light/shade, temperature, moisture, etc., and the areas in which woodlice are found.
* Produce a booklet about woodlice. Include information from books as well as from investigations.
* Produce a pamphlet which describes how to keep woodlice in the classroom. Include information from investigations.

▶ CURRICULUM LINKS

MATHEMATICS
Understand the notion of scale in maps and drawings. Draw an outline of the school grounds to a simple scale.

ENGLISH
Produce a pamphlet which describes how to keep woodlice in the classroom and includes information from investigations.

Paper

☐ 1 Which is the best disposable nappy?

☐ 9 Which is the best type of paper to use to make recycled paper?

☐ 2 Picnic time

☐ 8 Champion paper! Find out which is the strongest paper.

☐ 3 Science detectives

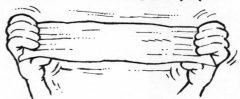

Paper

☐ 7 Consumer <u>Which</u> test. Find out which paper towel is the best.

☐ 4 Save-a-tree week

☐ 6 Biodegradable paper

☐ 5 Recycling paper

NAME:

Cross-curricular links

Paper

HISTORY

- Research into the history of paper making
- Find out about the development of printing through the ages
- Research writing styles through the centuries

MATHEMATICS

- Measuring paper dimensions - A4, A3, A2, A1
- How thick is paper and card?
- Best buys for school, comparing catalogue prices
- Wastepaper surveys in school and at home
- Tabulating information
- Bar graphs
- Area of paper
- Tangrams

TECHNOLOGY

- Design, make and test:
  - paper structures
  - paper bags
- Set up a mini-enterprise to make and sell paper products, e.g. notepads, origami models
- Design, produce and sell a class or school newspaper
- Newspaper layout and graphics
- Identify need in terms of handling wastepaper in the school and suggest strategies
- Create a system within the school or classroom for recycling paper and card

ENVIRONMENTAL EDUCATION

- Locate and produce maps of the area showing wastepaper collection points
- Research into recycling paper
- Carry out a wastepaper survey
- Design and put into practice methods of reducing the amount of paper used in school
- Design and use a system of recycling paper waste in school
- Paper production - afforestation, monocultures and associated ecological problems
- Different habitats and environments destroyed or created through tree planting

RE

- Communication in different religions, e.g. the Koran, Talmud, Bible, Dead Sea Scrolls

ART

- Making coloured paper
- Printing on paper, e.g. block printing, rollers, sponges
- Scrap-paper pictures
- Paper quilling
- Decorating paper
- Marbling

ENGLISH

- Survey of different uses for paper
- Analyse language used in books, leaflets, comics
- Use appropriate terminology from industry
- Write a report on the school's recycling project
- Write letters to manufacturers asking for information and samples of paper
- Use different styles of calligraphy
- Produce or edit a class newspaper

COMMUNITY LINKS

- Visits to:
  - a stationer's
  - a paper manufacturer
  - a printing works

- Visits from:
  - an author
  - a newspaper editor
  - a speaker on recycling
  - an artist
  - a cartoonist

MUSIC

- Paper instruments:
  - box guitars
  - straw pipes
  - pan pipes
  - shakers
  - papier-mâché maracas

▶ RESOURCES

collection of different types of paper, e.g. tissue paper, sugar paper, newspaper, writing paper, rice paper, waxed paper, greaseproof paper, glossy paper, computer paper
collection of fabrics
collection of paper and polystyrene cups

collection of paper towels
collection of water-based felt-tip pens
different types of disposable nappies
disposable plastic gloves
filter papers
food colouring
hand lenses
ice-cream cartons

J-cloths
net curtaining
net frames or deckles for paper-making
plant pots
plaster of Paris
plastic buckets
plastic washing-up bowls
potato masher
Quink ink

thermometers
tights
wooden bread tray
yoghurt pots

* camera
* second-hand liquidiser

93

Which is the best disposable nappy?

Most parents agree that the best disposable nappy is the one that does not leak.

Find a way of testing different nappies to find out which is the best.

Use a table for your results.

WHEN YOU HAVE FINISHED

Design and make a poster advertising the best nappy.

1 Which is the best disposable nappy?

Nappies are not normally found in primary classrooms! Two possible sources might be parents in the community who are willing to donate a few, or manufacturers. For the investigation it might be more economical to cut the nappies into as many pieces as possible rather than use whole nappies.

▶ USEFUL STARTING POINT

You could ask the children to carry out a survey of parents with babies or toddlers and canvas opinions about what makes a good disposable nappy and which brand they prefer. Their criteria will undoubtedly include:
- does not leak
- does not become soggy and cause discomfort.

▶ Focus

Measurements provide us with the evidence which is needed to decide not only 'which is best', but also 'how much better' one item or material is compared with others which have been tested.

During the planning stage, discuss what the children intend to do, encouraging them to consider:
- what to measure
- when to measure
- how to use the measuring equipment and, if a range of equipment is available, which equipment is most appropriate for their needs.

The focus here is on measuring how much water each type of nappy is able to absorb. There are several ways in which this can be done, some of which are more accurate than others, but they are all likely to involve measuring the **volume** of water at some stage. Measuring jugs are unlikely to provide the accuracy which is needed under these circumstances as the graduations on the scale are far too large. A measuring cylinder, however, has a more appropriate scale for this particular task, enabling the children to measure volume more accurately, and to deduce small differences in volume.

Teacher intervention might be needed to show the children how to use a measuring cylinder correctly. When taking measurements, eye level should be at the same as that of the liquid in the cylinder. The surface of the liquid in the measuring cylinder will appear curved (the curve is called the **meniscus**). Measurement should be made from the bottom of the meniscus as shown in the diagram.

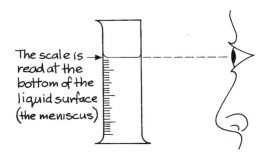

The scale is read at the bottom of the liquid surface (the meniscus)

▶ VARIABLES

The variables in this investigation could include:

Independent	Dependent	Control
Make of nappy	Amount of water which is absorbed or Amount which soaks through or Amount of water poured on before it begins to soak through	Amount of water poured onto nappy Time for the water to soak through Amount of nappy used

▶ FOLLOW-UP

The children could take a disposable nappy apart to find out which materials were used and whether they were put together in a particular way. They should consider the properties of the materials which are used - how are they suited to the purpose?

▶ COMMUNICATION

* Produce an advert for a nappy using the information from the investigation.
* Create packaging for a set of nappies. On the package explain why the nappies are absorbent.
* Annotate a diagram to describe how the nappies were tested.

▶ CURRICULUM LINKS

MATHEMATICS
Understand the relationship between units, e.g. millilitres and litres.

ENGLISH
Draw and annotate a diagram to show how the investigation was carried out.

Picnic time

2

Andrew has a problem.

He does not know which of these cups to use for hot drinks.

He does not want the soup to go cold too quickly.

Paper cup

Polystyrene cup

Carry out a fair test to find out which cup is best for hot drinks.

2 Picnic time

▶ USEFUL STARTING POINT

Discuss with the children why they think disposable cups are made of different materials and which cups (from a collection) they would use for hot drinks. Ask the children to think about how they would answer the question posed on the activity sheet, suggesting strategies for tackling the problem.

▶ Focus

When hot drinks are placed in cups the liquid in the cups is at a higher temperature than the surroundings, consequently the drinks lose heat energy. Some of the heat energy which is lost is absorbed into the air and because it is so spread out its effect is not noticed.

As a hot drink loses heat energy the temperature of the liquid falls. The more energy it loses the greater the fall in temperature. Some of the heat energy that is lost passes through the material of the cup.

Some materials allow heat to pass through them more easily than others. These are called **conductors**. Those materials which allow heat to pass through them slowly are called **insulators**.

One of the most important factors in this type of activity is whether children can recognise the need to allow the liquid sufficient time to cool. Unless a reasonable time is allowed for cooling, the difference in temperature fall may not be sufficient to make valid comparisons between the cups. This activity requires the children to measure a fall in temperature. This means that they must measure the temperature of the water in each cup when they begin their test and then again after some period of time (about five or six minutes). They then need to calculate the difference in temperature from the beginning to the end.

Children frequently make the mistake of measuring temperatures at the beginning and the end and then taking the higher temperature as the one which is best. Hence, if cup A begins at 27°C and ends at 22°C whilst cup B begins at 30°C and ends at 23°C, they take B to be the best because it finishes at the higher temperature. However, A falls 5°C whilst B falls 7°C and so, in fact, the best cup is A. This is a difficult idea and one where the children might need support and discussion.

The cup which has the smallest temperature fall (from start to finish) is the best for keeping things warm and is made from the best insulator.

▶ FOLLOW-UP

The children could design and make their own water-proof cup or container using paper. This will involve overcoming the problem of how to make the paper waterproof and how to construct it in a manner which avoids leaks. If several designs are made by different children, they can be used to carry out a fair test to find out which one is best. The children could also test a range of paper products from plates to tablecloths to find out which ones are the best.

▶ COMMUNICATION

* Draw and annotate a diagram to show how the investigation was carried out.
* Word-process a sequential account of the activity which includes reference to the data and conclusions reached.

▶ CURRICULUM LINKS

MATHEMATICS
Use subtraction to find the differences in temperature.

ENGLISH
Revise and redraft a report on the investigation and check the accuracy of spelling.

Science detectives

DID YOU KNOW THAT ...

The ink in some pens is made up of different colours.

The ink in a black pen can be separated into blue and pink colours.

We can find out how many different colours are in ink by dropping water onto an ink spot on filter paper.

Dropper

Drops of water

Ink spot

Filter paper

YOGHURT

Yoghurt pot

Vishni and Rachel have been trying to find out which of their felt-tip pens is made up of the most colours.

Try the experiment with your own felt-tip pens.

Use a table to record your results.

3 Science detectives

▶ USEFUL STARTING POINT

Ask the children to collect a range of inks, pens and felt-tip pens. The activity sheet introduces the technique of **chromatography**. Once the children have mastered this technique they can apply it in other situations. For example, the teacher might suggest to the children that they will be playing the role of scientific detectives. Activities such as chromatography need a context for the children to see the usefulness of this type of scientific technique. One context might be to ask the children to identify a piece of written work from someone in the class which no-one recognises as theirs. By testing the writing against the pens used in the classroom the children might be able to match the work with the pen that was used and so identify the writer.

▶ Focus

The children might at some point have noticed that when they spill water on a piece of paper with ink writing on it the ink spreads and a variety of colours can be seen. Many coloured materials contain several different coloured pigments. The different pigments cannot be separated by filtering or evaporation. When felt-tip pens are used on some types of paper (such as blotting paper or filter paper) and water is added, several colours may be seen to separate out at the edges. The process used to separate coloured pigments in this way is called **chromatography**. This process is used, for example, to find out which colouring agents are in food.

There are several methods children can use to separate colours. It is important to note that only water-based felt-tip ink will separate when water is used. Spirit-based pens should not be used. Quink ink is excellent for this activity, particularly black which provides a wide range of colours.

The results are known as **chromatograms**. Do introduce children to terms like this. Many will enjoy using the terminology and they should increasingly be made more aware that science has a specific language which is not difficult and can be accessible.

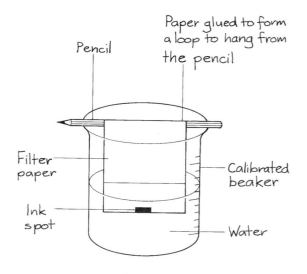

Pencil

Paper glued to form a loop to hang from the pencil

Filter paper

Ink spot

Calibrated beaker

Water

▶ FOLLOW-UP

The children could create their own detective file, in this way linking language with science. Within the file they could tell the story of an incident and describe how chromatography was used to solve a mystery. They could include chromatograms in the file as evidence.

▶ COMMUNICATION

* Produce a set of instructions, for another person to use and evaluate, describing how to make chromatograms.

* Create a detective's file which describes a mystery and includes the evidence (chromatograms).

▶ CURRICULUM LINKS

ENGLISH
Write a mystery story using the idea of chromatography in the storyline.

Save-a-tree week

DID YOU KNOW THAT ...

130 million trees are chopped down each year to provide paper for the United Kingdom.
This means about two trees are chopped down per person per year.

Carry out a paper survey.
Find out how much paper is used in your class each day for a week.

Talk with other people in your group.
How will you carry out your survey?
Use a table to help you.

Day	Amount of paper
Monday Tuesday	

How many different ways can you think of to save paper in the classroom? Make a list.

WHEN YOU HAVE FINISHED

Give a talk to the rest of your class about your survey.
Tell them about your ideas for saving paper.
Try out some ideas

4 Save-a-tree week

▶ USEFUL STARTING POINT

Provide the children with details of how much the school spends on paper each year. Discuss this amount in relation to other types of spending to put it into perspective, e.g. the amount spent on pencils, paints and other equipment. They might be surprised to find out how expensive card and sugar paper can be. Discuss the need to be careful about how paper is used, both in terms of cost and also the effects on the environment.

The activity sheet introduces the use of paper resources from an environmental perspective, providing some facts about how many trees are cut down in a year to provide paper in the UK. The annual paper consumption is equivalent to 130 million trees. This means that about two trees are felled per year per person in the country. Calculators could be used to find out how many trees are felled to provide paper for:
- the children in the class
- the pupils in the school
- the people in the village/town/city.

The children are then asked to carry out a survey within the classroom to find out how much paper is used every day. Using their data, they can calculate how much paper is used in a week, month or year by one child.

▶ Focus

Children need to appreciate that paper is made from trees (the wood is the raw material which is then processed to make the paper). Each year millions of trees are felled to provide the paper and card which we use. Trees help to maintain an ecological balance on the Earth's surface. They provide habitats for millions of small animals and plants. When trees are felled for paper production, these habitats are destroyed. Trees also help to maintain the balance of oxygen in the atmosphere by absorbing some of the carbon dioxide (the gas we breathe out) and replacing it with oxygen (the gas which all living things need).

Paper is expensive to produce. Large quantities of fossil fuels (non-renewable resources) and water are used in paper manufacture. The chemicals used in the paper-making process may be discharged into the rivers and oceans of the world, adding to pollution problems which already exist.

Environmental issues such as these are rarely simple, but children should be made increasingly aware of the possible damage to the natural word which results from our everyday actions and needs. At the same time, they need to recognise that there are two sides to every story, and they should also discuss the benefits of paper, from its use in schools, hospitals, in communication and in the employment of people in the paper manufacturing industry and other industries.

▶ FOLLOW-UP

Ask the children to think about how we could conserve paper and card. They might consider, for example:
- re-using cardboard boxes
- collecting newspapers and taking them to a recycling collection point
- using recycled paper products
- cutting spare paper from used paper and using it for notepads
- keeping card scraps
- creating a paper-sorting area where children put scrap paper in certain trays for re-use
- bringing scrap card and paper from home
- making better use of jotter pages
- deciding whether they really need paper or if there is an alternative, for example the chalkboard.

▶ COMMUNICATION

* Use a table to show how much paper is used daily in the class or school. The amount used could be quantified in a number of ways, e.g. by classifying and counting sheets, weighing, etc.
* Create a poster to tell other people why we should be recycling and using less paper.
* Produce a leaflet for other classes which explains how to reduce the amount of paper used in the classroom.

▶ CURRICULUM LINKS

MATHEMATICS
Select the materials and the mathematics to use for a task; check results and consider whether they are sensible.

ENGLISH
Interview a member of the class who has carried out a paper survey, asking suitable questions.

Recycling paper

Follow the instructions to make your own recycled paper.

① Tear newspaper into small pieces and put them into a plastic bowl. Add hand-hot water until the paper is covered.
Mash the paper with an old potato masher for about 15 minutes.
Drain off extra water.

② Gently push the frame into the pulp until it is covered.

Frame

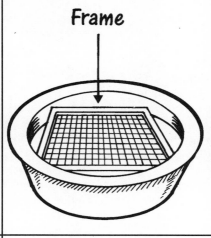

③ Lift the frame out and let the water drip off.

④ Tip the frame carefully onto a J-cloth laid on top of newspaper.

Newspaper

J-cloth

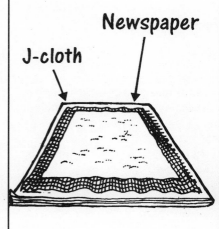

⑤ Make layers of pulp and J-cloths, like a sandwich.
Put a wooden board over the J-cloths and press on it to squeeze out extra water.
Leave the layers to dry.

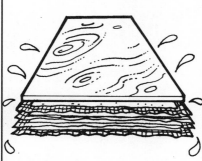

⑥ When dry, separate the layers to give you your sheets of recycled paper.

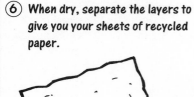

WHEN YOU HAVE FINISHED

Find out if your recycled paper is as strong as ordinary paper.

5 Recycling paper

This can be a messy activity. It is certainly time-consuming and children have to wait at least one day before they have a finished product. Some of the following suggestions might be useful.

- Set up a paper-making area within the classroom. Allow only small groups of children (twos or threes) to work in the area.
- Newsprint makes hands dirty and can mark clothing. Encourage the children to wear aprons, to roll up their sleeves and to wash their hands when they have finished tearing the sheets.
- The quality of recycled paper depends on what is used. Waste computer paper is excellent; newspaper is useful but the resulting recycled paper is grey.
- Paper pulps more easily if torn into small pieces.
- A liquidiser can be used to mash the pulp, but the process can ruin the blades and the appliance should not be used for food afterwards.
- The children will need a deckle. It is useful to have several of these available.

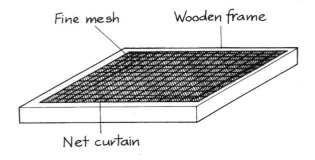

Fine mesh   Wooden frame

Net curtain

▶ Focus

Following on from the previous activity, the children should be made increasingly aware that some materials, including paper, can be processed and re-used. Most metals can be recycled. Glass can be recycled. Other waste materials which cannot be recycled can be burned and used to produce energy for heating, or for generating electricity.

By returning paper for recycling, we can reduce the demand for wood and protect some of the afforested areas of the Earth. However, the children should also be made aware of the fact that not all paper materials can be recycled. Some, such as paper containers with a plastic or wax coating, those with

metal liners and those with glue on them, cannot be recycled because the different materials cannot readily be separated from one another.

This activity requires the children to follow a set of instructions. The ability, and discipline, required to follow instructions carefully is an important skill which the children will use throughout their lives in many ways. It is also important that they recognise that instructions can be modified to suit a particular purpose. In this activity the children make paper using a basic recipe but they could be invited to modify the instructions to produce different effects. They could make these changes in a systematic way, and create a fair test to find out which changes produce the best result. For example, if they try to make scented paper, they might decide to divide the pulp into three or four separate containers and add a different type of ingredient to each amount of pulp. Once the paper is made, the children will need to decide how they can tell which is best.

▶ FOLLOW-UP

Encourage the children to ask further questions about their paper. They could, for example, suggest investigating:
- Does the amount of water affect the paper?
- Which is the best place for drying paper?
- Which is the best way to make coloured paper?
(Poster paint, ink, blackberry juice, the juice from pulped dandelion flower heads, tea leaves and coffee can all be used in the pulp to dye the paper.)
- Does the size of the torn paper affect the results?
- How can patterned paper be made?

▶ COMMUNICATION

* Use recycled paper to write and draw an explanation of how it was made. Include any problems encountered and the solutions.
* Take a set of photographs to show how to make recycled paper. Display them alongside a written or tape-recorded explanation.

▶ CURRICULUM LINKS

ENGLISH
Create a book describing how recycled paper is made. Use recycled paper for the book.

Biodegradable paper

DID YOU KNOW THAT ...

Things which rot are called biodegradable, for example potato peel, wool and bread. Aluminium cans and plastic bottles are non-biodegradable as they do not rot away.

David's group decided to bury pieces of paper to find out which type of paper rots the fastest.

> Talk with your friends.
> What do you think David's group did?
> Test your ideas.

THINK ABOUT

- What type of paper will you use?

- How much paper will you use?

- How will you bury the paper?

- Will you keep the soil wet or dry?

- How often will you look at the paper?

- How will you keep a record of what happens?

6 Biodegradable paper

▶ SAFETY

● This activity suggests burying paper in soil. Ensure that the soil is in a safe area, i.e. where animals are not exercised. Soil can transfer diseases. Children should always wear disposable gloves when handling soil, and should wash their hands immediately they are finished.

▶ USEFUL STARTING POINT

Discuss differences between biodegradable and non-biodegradable materials with the children. Biodegradable materials are capable of being broken down by bacteria. Paper, for example, is biodegradable. However, different types of paper will degrade at different rates - glossy magazine paper, for example, will take longer to break down than tissue paper.

Changes of this nature will take several weeks before it becomes really apparent that any change has taken place. It is important, however, that children experience long-term change as well as short-term change. It is equally important that children set up investigations which require observations and data collection over long periods of time. This activity provides the ideal opportunity for both. Warn the children not to expect results immediately and suggest that they make observations once or twice a week on a regular basis.

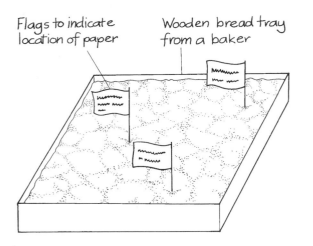

Flags to indicate location of paper

Wooden bread tray from a baker

Ask the children to think about what happens to paper in the environment. They might reply that it will be: torn; blown about; soaked in puddles or by rain; buried; subjected to a range of temperatures. Challenge the pupils to simulate some of these conditions in their investigation. Before the paper is buried the children need to consider how they will locate the samples in order to carry out regular observations.

VARIABLES

The variables in this investigation are:

Independent	Dependent	Control
Types of paper	Change in size in a set time or Change in colour or Change in texture	Size of buried items Bury in the same way Bury to the same depth Bury in the same area

▶ Focus

Much of the paper thrown into waste bins is mixed with other forms of waste and dumped in landfill sites (often old quarries). Over a period of time the paper decomposes, helped by the action of bacteria. Materials which decompose in this way are called **biodegradable**. Most naturally occurring materials such as wool and wood or materials which are derived from them, such as paper, are biodegradable.

Many manufacturers now produce biodegradable products. The children may have seen these advertised on television or in magazines. They may see evidence of them in their own homes in the form of soap powders, shampoos or chemicals used in the garden. Although these often cost more, they should do less harm to the environment. However, children should be encouraged to consider advertisements carefully and not take them for granted.

▶ FOLLOW-UP

With the children, brainstorm a set of questions arising from this investigation.
- Do larger pieces of paper degrade more slowly than smaller pieces?
- What happens to other materials, e.g. plastics, card, wood, fabric?
- How can we speed up or slow down the process?

▶ COMMUNICATION

* Produce a chart to record weekly the changes that take place in the paper. Include qualitative and quantitative observations.

▶ CURRICULUM LINKS

MATHEMATICS
Select the materials and the mathematics to use for a task; check results and consider whether they are sensible.

ENGLISH
Give a regular report to the rest of the class on the progress of the investigation.

7 Consumer <u>Which</u> test. Find out which paper towel is the best

▶ USEFUL STARTING POINT

Ask the children to make a collection of kitchen towels in order to carry out their own consumer *Which?* test on which type is best. They should keep a record of information such as:
- how many sheets of paper towel the packaging states there are
- the price of the paper towels
- whether the towels are made from recycled paper
- how many layers the paper towels contain.

This information could be used at a later stage to generate new questions, for example:
- Does the number of layers affect the amount of water a towel can mop up?
- Is recycled paper as good as other paper?
The information might also be used to decide which type of paper towel gives value for money.

Before the children start their investigation, encourage them to decide what their criteria for 'best' are.

▶ VARIABLES

The variables in this investigation are:

Independent	Dependent	Control
Type of paper towel	Volume of water	Size of paper towel Amound of water spilled Method of mopping up water

▶ Focus

It is important that children are offered similar investigations from time to time. This activity allows children to handle ideas in a context similar to that of the first investigation in this unit. With familiarity will come confidence and the teacher should challenge the children to use their knowledge and understanding from the first activity. It is particularly important that the children continue to make sure that they measure volume accurately, whether it is the dependent variable or a control variable where they make sure the same amount of water is spilled for all paper towels.

Ask the children to look at their results and place the paper towels in order from best to worst. Encourage them to suggest reasons why certain towels were better than others and then test their own ideas by carrying out a new set of investigations, for example:
- Does the thickness of the paper towel affect how much it mops up?

▶ COMMUNICATION

* Produce a table of results with samples of the paper towels displayed alongside.
* Produce a consumer report to display within the school so that parents can see how the investigation was carried out. Include the evidence which helped to decide which paper towel was the best.

▶ CURRICULUM LINKS

MATHEMATICS
Enter information in a simple database and construct and interpret a bar chart using information from the database.

ENGLISH
Give an oral report to the rest of the class describing how the investigation was carried out, the results and conclusions.

8 Champion paper! Find out which is the strongest paper

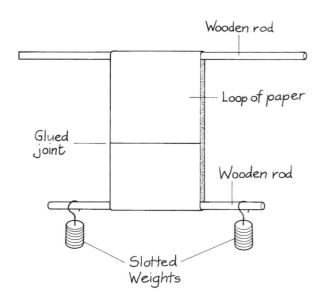

Wooden rod

Loop of paper

Glued joint

Wooden rod

Slotted Weights

▶ SAFETY

● When children are using masses ensure that they will not drop them onto toes or fingers. It may be advisable to place foam or a bucket filled with balls of newspaper underneath the masses.

▶ USEFUL STARTING POINT

Ask the children to make a collection of different types of paper. This might include some of the following:

tissue paper	sugar paper	newspaper
computer paper	writing paper	waxed paper
greaseproof paper	magazinepaper	rice paper

Ask the children to investigate which paper is the strongest. One of the most effective ways of tackling this is to hold the paper and place masses on it until it tears. This method is shown in the diagram opposite.

▶ VARIABLES

The relevant variables in this investigation are indicated below:

Independent	Dependent	Control
Type of paper	Weight needed to tear each paper	Amount of paper (area) Method of placing masses on the paper Method of holding paper

▶ Focus

This activity challenges the children to find a successful way of securing the paper in order to place or hang masses on it.
In all investigations the children should continually analyse and evaluate the effectiveness of their solutions. They should be encouraged to become increasingly more critical of the methods which are used. Effective questioning by the teacher can help in this process. For example the teacher might ask:
- Did you have any problems with this activity?
- Can you think of another way of holding the masses?
- If you could do the test again what would you change to improve it?
- Did other people have ideas that were not used? Do you think their idea would have worked?

▶ FOLLOW-UP

Ask the children to think about the investigation they have just carried out and to suggest other questions that they might try to answer, for example:

- If the layers of paper were doubled or trebled would it be two or three times as strong?

- If the size of the paper was two or three times bigger would the paper be stronger?

- Is the paper as strong when it is wet?

▶ COMMUNICATION

* Create a strip cartoon describing the investigation, including what was done, the results and conclusions.
* Annotate a diagram to show how the investigation was carried out.
* Create a booklet using a cartoon character to explain how the investigation was carried out.

▶ CURRICULUM LINKS

MATHEMATICS
Find areas by counting squares when calculating the size of paper.

ENGLISH
Take part in a group discussion into how the investigation should be carried out.

9 Which is the best type of paper to use to make recycled paper?

This activity uses the instructions for making paper from Activity 5.

▶ USEFUL STARTING POINT

Discuss the paper-making process with the children. They may already have come across it if they have carried out Activity 5. Ask the children to suggest how they might change the paper-making recipe to find out which paper is the best to use in the recycling process.

One of the most important changes, besides using different kinds of paper, would be to scale down the process to make smaller samples of recycled paper using, for example, newspaper, magazine paper, used sugar paper, used computer paper. The children will find there are differences between the different types of paper produced and invariably it is the computer paper that produces the better quality recycled paper.

VARIABLES

The variables in the investigation are:

Independent	Dependent	Control
Type of paper	Quality of recycled paper	Amount of paper used Method of making paper

▶ Focus

It is important for children to realise that they can change instructions to suit their own purposes. In this case the children might make smaller amounts of recycled paper in order to be able to compare different types of paper in the process.

In order to make their final evaluation they will have to decide on their own set of criteria for 'best'. These might include some of the following:
- colour
- smoothness
- can paint, ink, pencil, chalk, crayon be used successfully on the paper?
- does it dry quickly?
- strength
- absorbency.

At a later stage the children might decide that they wish to produce coloured paper. They could test a range of possible dyes from ink and paint to natural vegetable dyes such as onion, beetroot or blackberry. At this stage a pair of rubber gloves is an advantage to avoid unnecessary staining of the hands.

▶ COMMUNICATION

* Produce a report using samples of the recycled paper to explain why some types of paper are better for recycling than others.
* Reproduce the recipe for making the best paper, and tape-record the instructions.
* Create a recycling handbook which describes how to make paper and uses samples to show how pulping different types of paper produces a range of recycled papers.

▶ CURRICULUM LINKS

ENGLISH
Create a set of oral instructions on how to make recycled paper.

SUGGESTED ASSESSMENT OPPORTUNITIES - *Airborne*

	Activity	Attainment Target 1 (scientific investigation)			Attainment Targets 2—4 (knowledge and understanding)	
		Programme of study	Statement of attainment		Programme of study	Statement of attainment
Core Units	1	Activities should involve problems which can be solved qualitatively, but which increasingly allow for some quantification of the variables	1,3b		Pupils should explore different types of forces, including gravity	—
	2	Activities should involve variables to be controlled in the development of 'fair tests'	1,3c		Pupils should explore different types of forces, including gravity	—
	3	Activities should foster the interpretation of data and evaluation against the demands of the problem	1,3d		Pupils should explore different types of forces, including gravity	—
	4	Activities should involve problems which can be solved qualitatively, but which increasingly allow for some quantification of the variables	1,3b		Pupils should be introduced to the idea that the relative sizes and direction of forces can affect the movement of an object	4,2c 4,3c
	5	Activities should encourage systematic listing and recording of data, for example, in frequency tables and bar charts	1,4c		Pupils should have the opportunity to make regular, quantitative observations and keep records of weather	3,4d (part) 4,2c
	6	Activites should involve problems which can be solved qualitatively, but which increasingly allow for some quantification of the variables	1,3b		Pupils should explore friction and investigate the ways in which the speed of a moving object can be changed by the application of forces	4,3c
Supplementary Units	7	Activities should help them use and develop scientific knowledge and understanding	1,4a		Pupils should explore different types of forces and use measurements to compare their effects in, for example, moving things	4,2c 4,3c
	8	Activities should help them use and develop scientific knowledge and understanding	1,4a		Pupils should explore different types of forces and use measurements to compare their effects in, for example, moving things	4,2c 4,3c
	9	Activites should involve variables to be controlled in the development of 'fair tests'	1,3c		Pupils should investigate the factors that affect plant growth	2,3c 2,4c

NOTES

1. The activities in **Science in Action - 5 to 16** provide opportunities for assessment at a range of levels as indicated in the tables.

2. Most statements of attainment have several references to allow topics to be revisited and to ensure coverage of different aspects of the same topic.

SUGGESTED ASSESSMENT OPPORTUNITIES - *Toybox*

	Activity	Attainment Target 1 (scientific investigation)		Attainment Targets 2—4 (knowledge and understanding)	
		Programme of study	Statement of attainment	Programme of study	Statement of attainment
Core Units	1	Activities should help pupils to use and develop scientific knowledge and understanding	—	Pupils should explore friction	4,3c
	2	Activities should help pupils to use and develop scientific knowledge and understanding	—	Pupils should investigate the properties of magnetic and non-magnetic materials	4,2a
	3	Activities should help pupils to use and develop scientific knowledge and understanding	—	Pupils should investigate movement in a variety of devices, e.g. toys and models. They should be introduced to the idea of energy transfer.	4,4b
	4	Activities should help pupils to use and develop scientific knowledge and understanding	—	Pupils should have the opportunity to construct simple circuits	4,3a 4,4a
	5	Activities should help pupils to use and develop scientific knowledge and understanding	—	Pupils should have the opportunity to construct simple circuits	4,3a 4,4a
	6	Activities should help pupils to use and develop scientific knowledge and understanding	—	Pupils should investigate the formation of shadows and represent in drawings their ideas about how light varies in terms of brightness and shade	4,2d
Supplementary Units	7	Activities should encourage systematic listing and recording of data	1,3b 1,3c	—	—
	8	Actvities should encourage the raising and answering of questions	1,3a 1,3b 1,3c	Pupils should explore friction and investigate the ways in which the speed of an object can be changed	4,3c
	9	Activities should involve problems which can be solved qualitatively, but which increasingly allow for some quantification of variables	1,3a 1,3b	Pupils should explore different types of forces, including gravity	4,2c 4,3c

SUGGESTED ASSESSMENT OPPORTUNITIES - *The Lighthouse Keeper's Lunch*

	Activity	Attainment Target 1 (scientific investigation) Programme of study	Statement of attainment	Attainment Targets 2—4 (knowledge and understanding) Programme of study	Statement of attainment
Core Units	1	Activities should foster the interpretation of data and evaluation against the demands of the problem	1,4b 1,4c	Pupils should learn that sounds are heard because they travel to the ear	4,3d (part)
	2	Activities should help pupils to use and develop scientific knowledge and understanding	—	Pupils should learn about the reflection of both light and sound and relate this to everyday effects	4,3d (part) 4,4a 4,4d
	3	Activities should involve problems which can be solved qualitatively, but which increasingly allow for some quantification of the variables	1,3b 1,3c 1,4b	Pupils should explore different types of forces, including gravity	4,2c 4,3c
	4	Activities should encourage the raising and answering of questions and involve problems which may be solved qualitatively but which increasingly allow for some quantification of variables	1,3a 1,3b 1,3c 1,3d 1,4a 1,4b 1,4c	Pupils should be introduced to the idea that forces act in opposition to each other, that one force may be bigger than another or equal to it, and that the relative sizes and directions of forces can affect the movement of an object	4,2c 4,3c 4,4c
	5	Actvites should encourage the formation of testable hypotheses drawing on their developing knowledge and understanding	—	Pupils should investigate the factors involved in floating and sinking	4,4c
	6	Activities should promote the search for patterns in data	1,4c	Pupils should have the opportunity to make regular, quantitative observations and keep records of weather	3,4d
Supplementary Units	7	Activities should involve problems which can be solved qualitatively but which increasingly allow for some quantification of variables	1,3b 1,3c 1,4b	Pupils should explore friction	4,3c
	8	Activities should help to use and develop scientific knowledge and understanding	—	Pupils should explore the effects produced by shining light through such objects as lenses	—
	9	Activities should develop skills of using equipment and measurement, encouraging the pupils to make decisions about when, what and how to measure	1,3b 1,3c 1,4b	Pupils should investigate a number of different everyday materials, grouping them according to their characteristics	3,3a

SUGGESTED ASSESSMENT OPPORTUNITIES - *The Baker*

	Activity	Attainment Target 1 (scientific investigation)		Attainment Targets 2—4 (knowledge and understanding)	
		Programme of study	Statement of attainment	Programme of study	Statement of attainment
Core Units	1	Activities should involve problems which can be solved qualitatively but which increasingly allow for some quantification of the variables	1,3b 1,3c 1,4c	Pupils should investigate movement using a variety of devices, for example toys and models, and they should be introduced to the idea of energy transfer	4,4b
	2	Activities should involve problems which can be solved qualitatively but which increasingly allow for some quantification of the variables	1,4b 1,4c	Pupils should investigate the concepts of hot and cold in relation to body temperature	4,2b
	3	Activities should develop skills of using equipment and measurement, encouraging them to make decisions about when, what and how to measure	1,3b 1,3c 1,3d	Pupils should investigate the action of heat on everyday materials resulting in permanent change. These might include cooking activities	3,4b
	4	Activities should develop skills of using equipment and measurement, encouraging them to make decisions about when, what and how to measure	1,5b	Pupils should investigate the action of heat on everyday materials resulting in permanent change. These might include cooking activities	2,3a 3,2b 3,4b
	5	Activities should encourage the raising and answering of questions and foster the interpretation of data, and evaluation against the demands of the problem	1,3b 1,3c 1,3d	Pupils should investigate (and measure) the similarities and differences between themselves, animals and plants. They should investigate the key factors in the process of decay, such as temperature, moisture, air and the role of microbes	2,2a 2,3a 2,5d
	6	Activities should involve the use of secondary sources, as well as first hand observations	—	Pupils should learn about factors that contribute to good health, including diet and safe handling of food	2,2a 2,3a
Supplementary Units	7	—	—	Pupils should investigate movement in a variety of devices, for example toys and models which are self-propelled or driven and use motors, belts, levers and gears. They should be introduced to the idea that energy sources may be renewable or non-renewable	4,2c 4,4b
	8	Activities should involve the use of secondary sources, as well as first hand observations	—	They should explore ideas about the process of growth and reproduction	2,2a 2,3c 2,4a
	9	Activities should be within their everyday experience, provide opportunities to explore with increasing precision and involve the use of secondary sources, as well as first hand observations	1,2b 1,2c 1,3b 1,3c	Pupils should learn about factors that contribute to good health	2,2a 2,3a

SUGGESTED ASSESSMENT OPPORTUNITIES - *Animals*

	Activity	Attainment Target 1 (scientific investigation)			Attainment Targets 2—4 (knowledge and understanding)	
		Programme of study	Statement of attainment		Programme of study	Statement of attainment
Core Units	1	—	—		Pupils should develop an awareness and understanding of the necessity for sensitive collection and care of living things	2,2a 2,3a
	2	Activities should help them to use and develop scientific knowledge and understanding and involve the use of secondary sources as well as first hand observations	—		Pupils should have the opportunity to develop skills in identifying locally occuring species of animals and plants by making and using simple keys	2,2b 2,4b
	3	Activities should encourage systematic listing and recording of data, for example in frequency tables and bar charts	—		Pupils should have the opportunity to develop skills in identifying locally occurring species of animals by making and using simple keys	2,2b 2,4b
	4	Activities should encourage the raising and answering of questions and involve the use of secondary sources as well as first hand observations	—		Pupils should explore some aspects of feeding, support, movement and behaviour in relation to themselves and other animals	2,2a 2,2c 2,3a
	5	Activities should encourage the raising and answering of questions, encourage the systematic listing and recording of data and foster the interpretation of data, and evaluation against the demands of the problem	—		Pupils should explore and investigate at least two different habitats and the animals and plants that live there. They should find out how the animals and plants are suited to those habitats	2,2a 2,2c 2,3b 2,4c
	6	Activities should encourage the raising and answering of questions, encourage the systematic listing and recording of data and foster the interpretation of data, and evaluation against the demands of the problem	—		Pupils should be introduced to the idea that food chains are a way of representing relationships	2,4d
Supplementary Units	7	Activities should involve the use of secondary sources as well as first hand observations and foster the interpretation of data and evaluation against the demands of the problem	—		Pupils should find out how animals and plants are suited to their habitats and how they are influenced by environmental conditions, including seasonal and daily changes	2,3b 2,4c
	8	Activities should help pupils to use and develop scientific knowledge and understanding	—		Pupils should find out how animals and plants are influenced by environmental conditions	2,2a 2,3b 2,4c
	9	Activities should encourage the raising and answering of questions, require an increasingly systematic approach involving the identification and manipulation of variables and foster the interpretation of data and evaluation against the demands of the problem	1,3a 1,3b 1,3c 1,3d		Pupils should find out how animals and plants are suited to their habitats and how they are influenced by environmental conditions	2,2c 2,3b

SUGGESTED ASSESSMENT OPPORTUNITIES - *Paper*

	Activity	Attainment Target 1 (scientific investigation)		Attainment Targets 2 — 4 (knowledge and understanding)	
		Programme of study	Statement of attainment	Programme of study	Statement of attainment
Core Units	1	Activities should involve variables to be controlled in the development of a fair test and involve problems which may be solved qualitatively but which increasingly allow for some quantification of the variables	1,4b 1,4c	—	—
	2	Activities should involve variables to be controlled in the development of a fair test and involve problems which may be solved qualitatively but which increasingly allow for some quantification of the variables	1,4b 1,4c	Pupils should investigate changes that occur when familiar substances are heated and cooled. Properties (of materials) should be investigated and related to everyday uses	4,2b 3,3a
	3	Activities should help pupils to develop scientific knowledge and understanding	—	Pupils should explore ways of separating and purifying mixtures, such as ink, by using chromatography	3,5a (part)
	4	Activities should help pupils to use and develop scientific knowledge and understanding	—	Pupils should explore the origin of a range of materials in order to appreciate that some occur naturally while many are made from raw materials. They should study aspects of the local environment affected by human activity and consider the benefits and detrimental effects of these activities	2,3b 3,3b
	5	Activities should encourage the raising and answering of questions and require an increasingly systematic approach involving the identification and manipulation of variables	1,3b 1,3c 1,4b 1,4c	Pupils should explore the origin of a range of materials in order to appreciate that some occur naturally while many are made from raw materials. They should study aspects of the local environment affected by human activity and consider the benefits and detrimental effects of these activities	2,3b
	6	Activities should require an increasingly systematic approach involving the identification and manipulation of key variables	1,3b 1,3c	Pupils should study the effects of pollution on the survival of living things and they should build on their investigations of decay and consider significant features of waste disposal	2,3b
Supplementary Units	7	Activities should involve variables to be controlled in the development of a fair test and involve problems which may be solved qualitatively but which increasingly allow for some quantification of the variables	1,3b 1,3c 1,3d 1,4b 1,4c 1,4d	—	—
	8	Activities should involve variables to be controlled in the development of a fair test and involve problems which may be solved qualitatively but which increasingly allow for some quantification of the variables and encourage pupils to appraise their investigations and suggest improvements to their methods	1,3b 1,3c 1,3d 1,4b 1,4c 1,4d	Pupils should explore different types of forces and compare their effects	4,3c 4,4c
	9	Develop skills of using equipment and measurement, encouraging them to make discussion about when, what and how to measure	1,3b 1,3c 1,3d 1,4b 1,4c	—	—

114